Ever Reforming

Dispensational Theology and the Completion of the Protestant Reformation

Dr. Andy Woods

DISPENSATIONAL
PUBLISHING HOUSE, INC.

This book was compiled with the assistance of Paul J. Scharf, editor in chief of Dispensational Publishing House.

Printed in the U.S.A.

First Edition, Second Printing, 2018

ISBN: 978-1-945774-19-5

Dispensational Publishing House, Inc.
PO Box 3181
Taos, NM 87571

www.dispensationalpublishing.com

Ordering Information:
Quantity sales. Special discounts are available on quantity purchases by churches, associations, and others. For details, contact the publisher at the address above.

Orders by U.S. trade bookstores and wholesalers. Please contact the publisher:
Tel: (844) 321-4202

2 3 4 5 6 7 8 9 10 1

This book Ever Reforming *is dedicated to Richard "Dick" Lane. He epitomizes what it means to be a true friend, ministry colaborer and fellow lover of truth. I praise God daily that He, in His sovereignty, allowed our paths to cross.*

Table of Contents

Foreword

Recently my wife and I had the incredible privilege of touring the sights that remain from the days of the Lutheran Reformation in Germany. We spent six exhausting but inspiring days remembering what happened a month shy of 500 years ago—touring places such as Eisleben, Eisenach, Erfurt and, of course, Wittenberg, Worms and the Wartburg Castle.

On the day of our flight home from Frankfurt, we were met by a very important person—the limousine driver who transported us from the hotel to the airport.

We knew little about this man, although we enjoyed his company for the short trip, and he took good care of us. His part in getting us home was instrumental—even necessary—although insufficient.

I suppose that there were other ways that we might have gotten to the airport, but this was the way that was selected for us by the tour company. Knowing of no direct alternatives in this foreign place, we obviously accepted the offer.

That driver's assistance was so crucial that, in one sense, we might say that we could not have made it home without his help.

In a limited way, this is an illustration of the work of Luther and the Reformers themselves. Their efforts were not ultimately sufficient, but they were fundamentally necessary. Certainly, God could have brought about such a work as the Protestant Reformation in numerous other ways—but this was the means that He chose to use. He even worked through men with great weaknesses in order to display this truth:

> God has chosen the foolish things of the world to shame the wise, and God has chosen the weak things of the world to shame the things which are strong, and the base things of the world and the despised God has chosen, the things that are not, so that He may nullify the things that are, so that no man may boast before God. (1 Cor. 1:27-29)

In this new volume done in honor of the 500th anniversary of the beginning of the Protestant Reformation, Dr. Andy Woods does a masterful job of explaining that, humanly speaking, we would not be here doing the things that we are engaged in today were it not for Luther and the Reformers. Yet Woods communicates clearly that the Reformers began an incomplete revolution—the progress of which continued to be advanced through the teachings of traditional dispensationalism, with many tasks still remaining to be completed even now.

We offer this new book in the hope, and with the prayer, that it will inform, inspire and motivate faithful believers to lead the visible church of Jesus Christ to new heights of knowledge and obedience in this late and dark hour.

We present it on the basis of the same truth that motivated the Reformers:

> For the vision is yet for the appointed time;
> It hastens toward the goal and it will not fail.
> Though it tarries, wait for it;
> For it will certainly come, it will not delay.
>
> Behold, as for the proud one,
> His soul is not right within him;
> But the righteous will live by his faith. (Hab. 2:3-4)

Paul J. Scharf
Oct. 31, 2017
Soli Deo Gloria – To God Alone Be Glory!

Acknowledgments

The genesis of this book was an invitation by Dr. David Reagan of Lamb and Lion Ministries to contribute a short article on the significance of the Protestant Reformation's relationship to Bible prophecy to his ministry's magazine. Thus, this article appeared in the edition of *Lamplighter* magazine commemorating the 500th-year-anniversary of the launching of the Protestant Reformation.[1] This article was then elongated into an academic format and was included as one of many scholarly articles in the book *Forged from Reformation*.[2] Most of the original citations used in the present work first appeared in this academic article. I was then invited to be a teacher on a Reformation cruise touring the original Reformation places, such as Wittenberg, Germany, by Bill Perkins of Compass Ministries. It was on this trip that I learned even more of the Protestant Reformation that I had written about in my articles. Upon my return, I launched a 14-week Sunday School series at my home church, Sugar Land Bible Church in Sugar Land, Texas, about the Protestant Reformation.[3] Paul Scharf of Dispensational Publishing House then took these messages and compiled them into the present work that is aimed at the laity. The present work is not only longer and contains sources not included in my prior articles, but it is also written in an entirely

1 Andy Woods, "A Failure of the Reformation," *Lamplighter* November–December 2017, pp. 8-12.

2 Andy Woods, "The Protestant Reformation: An Important and yet Incomplete Hermeneutical Reformation," in *Forged from Reformation: How Dispensational Thought Advances the Reoformed Legacy*, ed. Christopher Cone and James I. Fazio (El Cajon, CA: Southern California Seminary Press, 2017), pp. 227-63.

3 This series can be accessed in audio, video and written transcript format in the sermon archives section of the Sugar Land Bible Church website (www.slbc.org). Go to the series entitled, "Protestant Reformation."

different format and style. I praise the Lord for His sovereignty in ordering my steps so that the present book, *Ever Reforming*, can be a blessing to the present generation as they grow in their understanding of the Protestant Reformation's significance.

Introduction

I recently traveled to Germany twice during this 500th anniversary year of the Reformation. I stood at places like the door of the Castle Church in Wittenberg, Germany, where Martin Luther nailed his 95 theses.

You see, on Oct. 31, 1517—500 years ago—this monk, priest and professor, Martin Luther, triggered a chain reaction that was felt all throughout Europe. Despite the historical license that is often taken with these events, we need to understand that what Luther was really trying to do was to begin a conversation.

This was actually a common way of starting a dialogue or a dispute in Luther's day, and I think that he was surprised—more than anyone else—when the Roman Catholic Church, the only church of the day, eventually denounced him as a heretic.

But God worked sovereignly and strategically through these events, and it set off that reaction that we call the Protestant Reformation. We today are enjoying the fruit of that Reformation 500 years ago, but most Christians do not know much about it because we do not get a lot of historical teaching in our churches.

I hope that this book will fill in the gaps so that you will understand what happened 500 years ago—how God used these men, and especially how they put into motion a method of interpretation, called the literal, grammatical, historical method, which subsequent generations took and applied to the entirety of the Bible.

In fact, we would not have the theology that we have today were it not for God's initial work through the Protestant Reformers.

A Partial Restoration

The Protestant Reformers had a far-reaching impact, but they brought about only a partial restoration.

People have a tendency to place these Reformers on a pedestal and act like they completed the revolution, which they did not. Reformed theology, which was birthed out of the churches begun by the Reformers, has not completed that revolution, either. It would be up to other Christians to take the method that the Protestant Reformers used and complete that revolution by applying it to the whole Bible.

Why was the Protestant Reformation only a partial restoration? It was because they used the literal method of interpreting the Bible selectively. But, had they not given us that methodology—this great blueprint—at all, subsequent generations could not have come along and applied it consistently.

Stop and think for a moment: What in the world has God been doing since the closing of the New Testament canon? There have been almost 2,000 years of church history since that time, and we will try to put those pieces together—highlighting and emphasizing specifically what the Protestant Reformers accomplished 500 years ago.

But you cannot appreciate what the Reformers accomplished at all until you understand all that needed to be retrieved. You cannot appreciate a solution until you first understand the problem.

CHAPTER 1

The Early Church

We must understand what the apostles handed off to the first generation of Christians—and what the early church believed for its first 200 years.

The New Testament's Interpretation of Prophecy

The canon of Scripture officially shut when the Apostle John completed the book of Revelation in 95 A.D.

Now, we can tell from looking at various Biblical writers that when New Testament characters interpreted the Old Testament, particularly as it relates to the issue of the kingdom of God, they always took Bible prophecy at face value.

I am using Bible prophecy as a bellwether, because if you can spiritualize or allegorize away Bible prophecy, it will not be long until you spiritualize and allegorize away the rest of the Scriptures.

Notice how seriously Jesus took Old Testament prophecies concerning the kingdom:

> And Jesus said to them, "Truly I say to you, that you who have followed Me, in the regeneration when the Son of Man will sit on His glorious throne, you also shall sit upon twelve thrones, judging the twelve tribes of Israel." (Matt. 19:28)

Jesus is speaking about the Davidic throne, which is described in 2 Samuel 7:12-16. He took it literally—He believed in an earthly kingdom that would arrive here one day. There is no hint that He spiritualized or reinterpreted this prophetic concept.

Likewise, the Apostle Paul stated in Romans 11:25-27:

> For I do not want you, brethren, to be uninformed of this mystery—so that you will not be wise in your own estimation—that a partial hardening has happened to Israel until the fullness of the Gentiles has come in; and so all Israel will be saved; just as it is written,
>
> "The Deliverer will come from Zion,
> He will remove ungodliness from Jacob."
> "This is My covenant with them,
> When I take away their sins."

Notice that Paul says that Israel's hardening is *partial.* He is very clear that God is going to fulfill all of His purposes and His program through the nation of Israel. The verses that he quotes at the end are references to the various covenants that God made with the physical descendants of Abraham, Isaac and Jacob.

Consider also Revelation 5:10:

> You have made them *to be* a kingdom and priests to our God; and they will reign upon the earth.

Where will these believers reign? Will they just be strumming harps in the clouds? No—"they will reign upon the earth."

So we can see that the New Testament Biblical speakers and writers, including Jesus (as recorded by Matthew), Paul and John, all took Bible prophecy very literally and seriously. There is no hint anywhere that these prophecies would be fulfilled in any sense other than their literal sense. When you close the New Testament, this is the spirit and attitude that you have.

This mindset was handed off like a baton to the first generation of Christians after the apostles left the scene.

Antioch of Syria

To understand all that was going to unfold through the first 1,500 years of church history prior to the Reformation, we need to travel first to a city called Antioch of Syria.

That name should ring a bell for you.

Acts 11:25-26 states:

> And he left for Tarsus to look for Saul; and when he had found him, he brought him to Antioch. And for an entire year they met with the church and taught considerable numbers; and the disciples were first called Christians in Antioch.

Christians began to proliferate numerically here in the northern tip of Israel. Prior to this time, believers in the Lord Jesus Christ were not even called *Christians*. They had been known by names such as *the Way* (Acts 9:2; 22:4; 24:14). But these people acted so much like Jesus in terms of their moral character that people began to call them *Christians*.

Antioch thus becomes a big deal in Bible history. In fact, you can trace apostolic succession back to Antioch.

Paul launched all three of his missionary journeys from Antioch—going to southern Galatia; then to Greece and Asia Minor; then ultimately all the way to Rome. You will find the importance of this city in Acts 13:1-3; 14:26-28; 15:35-41; and 18:22-23.

Antioch is very significant. If you want to understand the way that the apostles think, you must study their students at Antioch. We can trace the Apostle Paul's ministry back to Antioch.

In fact, in terms of what it taught, Antioch became a bellwether for the early church and the apostolic teaching. When the apostles left the scene, a school was developed there—the school of Antioch. We might call it a seminary. The people there stood for the literal interpretation of the Bible.

Now, the Protestant Reformation ultimately brought us back to Antioch. But first we need to see the foundation which was in place there, and what was lost.

Antioch was known for its embracement and advocacy of literal interpretation. Premillennial scholar George Peters makes this clear through his citation of early church father Irenaeus (A.D. 125–202).

> The literal, grammatical interpretation of the Scriptures must . . . be observed in order to obtain a correct understanding. . . . The primitive church occupied this position, and Irenaeus . . . gives us the general sentiment . . . when he says of the Holy Scriptures: "that what the understanding can daily make use of, what it can easily know, is that which lies before our eyes, unambiguously, literally, and clearly in Holy Writ."[4]

Yes, the school of Antioch stood for literal interpretation—even when they came to the area of Bible prophecy. And from that school came a theological system known as *premillennialism*.

The word *millennium* is not found in Scripture, but we find the basis for the idea behind it in Revelation 20:1-10. While the term is not used, the concept is found there. Our word *millennium* comes from the Latin, which was the language used by theologians from the third century of church history onward, and it means *a thousand years*. The Greek word for this millennial belief system is *chiliasm* (from the Greek word for *thousand*, which is used six times in Rev. 20:1-10), and the students at Antioch were called *chiliasts*.

The concept of premillennialism is that Jesus will come back to the Earth first, and then the millennium will begin after that.

How did these people reach that conclusion? They did so by taking Bible prophecy literally—as Paul, John and Jesus did.

If you look at the state of world today, it is obvious that we are not in the millennium. The Bible speaks of this day as a period when there will not be any war or any starvation.

Isaiah 2:4 says of that time:

> And they will hammer their swords into plowshares and their spears into pruning hooks.
> Nation will not lift up sword against nation,
> And never again will they learn war.

4 George N. H. Peters, *The Theocratic Kingdom*, 3 vols. (New York: Funk & Wagnalls, 1884; reprint, Grand Rapids: Kregel, 1952), 1:47.

This can only happen after Christ returns—which is the concept behind *premillennialism*, which the school of Antioch was all about. Premillennialism is the outworking of the literal interpretation of the whole Bible.

This is the mindset that was passed from the apostles themselves to the first generation of Christians, and it dominated the church for its first two centuries.

Justin Martyr, who lived from about 100 to 160 A.D., represented the Antoichene mindset, and made an astounding statement in this regard:

> But I and every other completely orthodox Christian feel certain that there will be a resurrection of the flesh, followed by a thousand years in the rebuilt, embellished, and enlarged city of Jerusalem as was announced by the prophets Ezekiel, Isaiah, and the others.[5]

Justin Martyr believed that Jerusalem would again one day be the center of the world—and that Jesus Christ would rule over the world from that city during the kingdom age.

Notice the importance that Justin Martyr placed on the literal interpretation of prophecy. He said that you have to believe this to be an *orthodox Christian.* How different this is from the ecumenical mindset of our day! We often hear that Christians are free to agree to disagree on their views of Bible prophecy. But based on this quotation, I believe that the early church was premillennial, and that all other views were considered heretical. This is the mindset that began in the school of Antioch.

Here is a quote about the first generation of Christians following the apostles, after the canon of Scripture was closed, from the great church historian, Philip Schaff:

> The most striking point in the eschatology of the ante-Nicene age (A.D. 100–325) is the prominent chiliasm, or millenarian-

5 Justin Martyr, *Dialogue with Trypho*, chap. 80.

> ism, that is the belief of a visible reign of Christ in glory on earth with the risen saints for a thousand years, before the general resurrection and judgment. It was indeed not the doctrine of the church embodied in any creed or form of devotion, but a widely current opinion of distinguished teachers, such as Barnabas, Papias, Justin Martyr, Irenaeus, Tertullian, Methodius, and Lactantius.[6]

Now people will ask, "If premillennialism is true, how come it is not found in the Apostle's Creed or the Nicene Creed?"

But you need to understand something—the creeds and confessions of Christendom were not designed in the way that we as a church would put together a doctrinal statement today.

Churches today put doctrinal statements together to say exactly what they believe. But the early church did not think that way. In fact, they did not have to do it that way—because everyone believed the correct doctrine.

Creeds and confessions came about as a response to heretics. They were never designed to be a sum total of Christian truth, but they were intended to respond to heretics at specific points.

One of the heretics that arose early on was a man named Arius. He basically taught what the modern-day Jehovah's Witnesses teach—that Jesus was a created being. In fact, Arius even had a song which states that there was a time in which Jesus did not exist. He believed that God the Father created God the Son. When the Jehovah's Witnesses show up at your door and try to convince you that Jesus is a created being, they are simply teaching recycled Arianism. And the early church responded to that heresy through the Nicene Creed.

It teaches that Christ was "begotten, not made." But the Nicene Creed was never supposed to include everything that the church believed. It was written for the purpose of responding to Arius on a particular point.

---

6 Philip Schaff, *History of the Christian Church*, vol. 2, *Ante-Nicene Christianity AD 100–325* (1910; repr., Grand Rapids, MI: Eerdmans, 1976), p. 614.

Therefore, we did not see creeds and confessions come about in the early church until major heresies began to emerge. They were not needed because every Christian believed the correct doctrine—or else they were not considered Christians.

That is why premillennialism, or chiliasm, does not show up in the early church creeds. This statement by Schaff is very important. It is telling us that—even though there was no formal creed, because creeds were given later to respond to heretics who had not yet arisen—chiliasm or premillennialism was the *reigning sentiment* that everyone believed. It was dominant!

We see that specifically in this quotation from Edward Gibbon, who wrote the historical treatise called *The History of the Decline and Fall of the Roman Empire*. As far as I know, Gibbon did not have a Christian bone in his body, but he attempted to be an honest historian.

In one of Gibbon's books, called *The History of Christianity*, he made a statement about what the early church believed:

> The ancient and popular doctrine of the Millennium was intimately connected with the second coming of Christ. As the works of the creation had been finished in six days, their duration in their present state, according to a tradition which was attributed to the prophet Elijah, was fixed to six thousand years. By the same analogy it was inferred, that this long period of labor and contention, which was now almost elapsed, would be succeeded by a joyful Sabbath of a thousand years; and that Christ, with the triumphant band of the saints and the elect who had escaped death, or who had been miraculously revived, would reign upon earth till the time appointed for the last and general resurrection. . . . The assurance of such a Millennium was carefully inculcated by a succession of fathers from Justin Martyr, and Irenaeus, who conversed with the immediate disciples of the apostles, down to Lactantius, who was preceptor to the son of Constantine. Though it might not be universally received, it appears to have been the reigning sentiment of the orthodox

> believers; and it seems so well adapted to the desires and apprehensions of mankind, that it must have contributed in a very considerable degree to the progress of the Christian faith.[7]

This doctrine is exactly what Jesus had taught in Matthew 19:28, what Paul said in Romans 11:25-27 and what John said in Revelation 5:10.

And who are these *fathers* that Gibbon is talking about? This is the first generation of Christians after the apostles left the scene. What he is saying is that these early church fathers have a direct line back to the apostles themselves. That is why the school of Antioch is so important—because you can trace apostolic succession back to Antioch.

And notice these key words of Gibbon: "It appears to have been the reigning sentiment of the orthodox believers." In other words, this idea of the literal interpretation of Bible prophecy was so dominant in the minds of the earliest Christians that they did not even see the need to formulate a creed at all.

Another reputable historian, Jesse Forest Silver made the following statement concerning the beliefs of the church in the years immediately after the apostles had left the scene. He says of the apostolic fathers that:

> They expected the return of the Lord in their day. . . . They believed the time was imminent because the Lord had taught them to live in a watchful attitude.[8]

I take this to mean that the early church believed very strongly—not only in premillennialism, but also in pretribulationalism. This is the idea that Jesus Christ is coming back for the church before the tribulation period starts.

Now did they have in-depth flowcharts like we have today, explaining all of these things in detail? No—because it is very difficult to put together your theological flowcharts when a man like Nero is trying to cut your head

---

7 Edward Gibbon, *History of Christianity* (NY: Eckler, 1916), pp. 141-44.

8 Jesse Forest Silver, *The Lord's Return: Seen in History and in Scripture as Premillennial and Imminent* (NY: Revell, 1914), pp. 62-64.

off. They did not have the blessings and luxuries that we enjoy today. They were fighting for their very lives to avoid prison or martyrdom. Yet, according to Silver, they believed in the imminent return of Jesus Christ. They saw that as the next event on the prophetic horizon. They were looking for Jesus Christ—not the antichrist.

Now where did they get this idea that Jesus could come back at any moment? They got it directly from the apostles, who themselves received it directly from Christ

Concerning the Ante-Nicene Fathers, Silver stated:

> By tradition they knew the faith of the apostles. They taught the doctrine of the imminent and pre-millennial return of the Lord.[9]

So they believed in *imminency*—that Christ can come back at any moment—and they believed in *chiliasm*, which is the idea of a 1,000-year kingdom established here on planet Earth.

What you must recognize is that this was the state of Christianity for the first two centuries of church history. Unless you understand that foundation, you cannot really comprehend what was lost. And unless you realize what was lost you cannot understand the work that God did in church history to raise up people like Martin Luther, and others, to restore what had been lost.

This is why I am not starting this study with the Protestant Reformation itself. I am starting at the very beginning—because unless you appreciate that beginning, and the foundation that was laid, and the baton that was handed off, you will not have any concept as to what God did through a monk named Martin Luther in 1517.

So what went wrong? What happened? Where did the shift away from literal interpretation originate?

We will find the answers to those questions in the next chapter.

---

9 Ibid.

CHAPTER 2

The Alexandrian Eclipse

It is important to realize that it is unlikely that I would have the privilege of writing this book—or that you would have the opportunity to read it—were it not for the move of God 500 years ago that we call the Protestant Reformation.

Yet it is difficult to understand the Protestant Reformation unless you understand what the apostles handed off to the early church—and what a subsequent generation of Christians lost, that needed to be recovered much later.

We have seen that the apostolic teaching was embodied by the students of the school at Antioch, where the Apostle Paul and others had ministered so strongly.

But down south, in a place called Alexandria, Egypt, a rival school to Antioch was started, which basically said that the literal interpretation of Scripture need not be the rule.

They saw Bible prophecy as being symbolic and metaphorical, and they developed what is called the *allegorical method* of interpretation. And once they spiritualized away Bible prophecy it was not long until the rest of Christianity was spiritualized, as well.

You see, if you cannot believe in a future resurrection of the body, then maybe even Jesus Himself did not come out of the grave in a real, physical body.

That is the type of thinking that was presented to the students at Alexandria. And, sadly, although Antioch had been dominant for 200 years, Alexandria ultimately won the day. The *reigning sentiment* of Jesus and the apostles and the first generation of Christians was eclipsed (hence the title for this chapter). It brought in this time that many call the *dark ages*, and this is exactly what Luther was trying to drag us out of. God raised up Luther more than 1,000 years after the literal interpretation of the Bible had been dismissed through the influence of Alexandria.

Paul's Warnings and Predictions

But before we start explaining that in depth, let us remember how the Apostle Paul, when completing his third missionary journey, warned the elders from the church at Ephesus in a harbor town called Miletus. He was a shepherd speaking to shepherds—about how to be a shepherd. And Ephesus was the key church at that point!

If you want to understand a proper philosophy of ministry, I would encourage you to read Acts 20. It ought to impact everything that we do as we seek to serve the Lord and His church. And listen to what Paul said in the midst of it:

> Therefore be on the alert, remembering that night and day for a period of three years I did not cease to admonish each one with tears. (Acts 20:31)

Paul had been warning these men for three years—to the point of tears—about what would happen when he and the rest of the apostles would leave the scene. He makes a prediction when he states:

> I know that *after my departure* savage wolves will come in among you, not sparing the flock; and *from among your own selves* men will arise, *speaking perverse things*, to draw away the disciples after them. (Acts 20:29-30; italics added)

This prediction is fleshed out in another book that Paul wrote—his final book—2 Timothy.

Now these words probably put the fear of God into some of these elders, because what he was saying was that some of them were going to turn in a theologically wrong direction after Paul left the church. This significant congregation would begin to drift under the influence of Alexandria. Now fortunately this did not happen for a couple of centuries—but it did happen.

Notice that Paul warned these elders of a two-pronged attack: *Savage wolves* are false teachers who would bring an external theological attack against the church. But then he describes an internal attack ("and from among your own selves").

The *perverse things* that Paul spoke of, which would come from both inside and outside of the church, are ideas that are contrary to that which was taught by Jesus, the apostles and the school of Antioch.

If you attempt to maintain the Biblical standards, you may well be called a hyper-literalist or a fundamentalist, a flat-earther, right-wing or narrow-minded. Through such derision and name calling the false teachers would seek to remove the church from apostolic teaching.

And that is exactly what happened in Alexandria, Egypt. As we have seen, there is much apostolic succession in Antioch. But there was none in Alexandria. No apostles had any connection whatsoever, that we know of, to Alexandria. That automatically tells you which school of thought you ought to follow if there is ever a dispute between these schools. Yet, sadly, the school that had no connection to the apostles began to dominate during the dark ages.

This city in northern Africa was home to the great Royal Library of Alexandria, and the city was known for its academics and scholarship. God, in His sovereignty, later allowed that library to be burned down. But just because the library was destroyed does not mean that the ideas formulated in Alexandria did not begin to dominate.

So, what were they teaching in Alexandria that was so wrong?

Allegorization

The school in Alexandria began to teach the allegorization of the Bible, as opposed to its literal interpretation. Allegorization is the idea that what the text says is really not what is important; rather, the theory goes, we can use the text of the Bible to teach something other than what we find in the actual text of the Bible. The interpreter uses the text of the Bible to bring in a higher meaning, which sounds much more spiritual. But only you—the allegorist—can really know what that meaning is.

Allegorization uses the language of the text to bring in a higher spiritual meaning. One of the great allegorists who influenced the school of Alexandria was named Philo. This process had actually started in Judaism, shortly before the time of Christ. Philo was born just a few years earlier than Jesus, and Philo is one of the men who introduced the allegorical method of interpretation.

Bernard Ramm states:

> The outstanding Jewish allegorist was Philo. . . . He was a thoroughly convinced Jew. To him the Scriptures (primarily in the Septuagint version) were superior to Plato and Greek philosophy. . . . Yet, he had a great fondness for Greek philosophy, especially Plato and Pythagoras. By a most elaborate system of allegorizing he was able to reconcile for himself his loyalty to his Hebrew faith and his love for Greek philosophy.[10]

To give you an example, Philo would take Genesis 2:11-14, which talks about four rivers in Eden—the Pishon, the Gihon, the Tigris and the Euphrates—and he would supply them with a higher, more spiritual sounding meaning. The higher meaning, he said, is that these rivers really represent four parts of the soul. Now, would that not really be more interesting than listening to a boring sermon about four rivers? Initially, the allegorist sounds so much more spiritual—and academic.

Ronald Diprose explains how Philo began to influence the church:

> Clement of Alexandria (c. 155–c. 220) was unashamedly a Christian Platonist and as such he quoted from Plato, and indeed from other philosophers, with the same ease as he quoted from the Hebrew Scriptures and the New Testament. Moreover,

10 Bernard Ramm, *Protestant Biblical Interpretation*, 3rd rev. ed. (Grand Rapids: Baker, 1970), p. 27.

he interpreted the Bible in light of Platonic concepts. . . . His dependence upon Plato is further evident in a speculative passage in which the Jews feature as "helpers" while the Christians are considered "fit to rule." Origen continued the Alexandrian tradition of interpreting the Bible in a way which harmonized with Greek philosophy.[11]

This is truly the origin of *replacement theology*—the idea that the church has permanently replaced Israel in the plan of God.

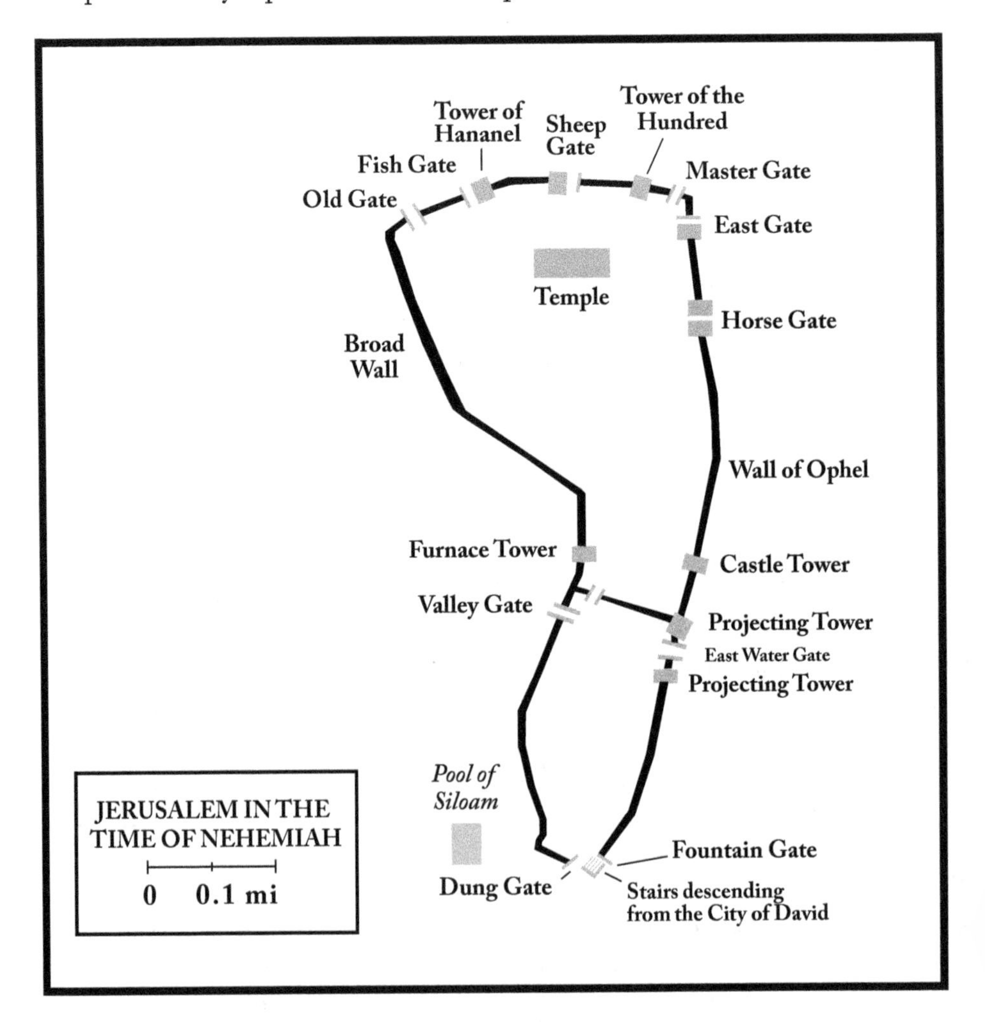

11 Ronald E. Diprose, *Israel in the Development of Christian Thought* (Rome: IBEI, 2000), pp. 157-58.

Another passage that is used this way even today is found in Nehemiah 3. It describes the gates in the wall around the city of Jerusalem, which was rebuilt by Nehemiah and the people that he led back from the Babylonian captivity, in the fifth century before Christ.

Nehemiah 3:1 describes "the Sheep Gate." Now, the allegorist will be tempted to think that the Sheep Gate represents Jesus because John the Baptist said about Him, "Behold, the Lamb of God!" (John 1:36; cf. v. 29).

Nehemiah 3:3 speaks of "the Fish Gate." Certainly, this could represent evangelism, could it not, since Jesus told us to be "fishers of men" (Matt. 4:19; Mark 1:17)?

In Nehemiah 3:6 we find "the Old Gate." To the allegorist, this relates to conversion—because, for the Christian, "the old things passed away; behold, new things have come" (2 Cor. 5:17).

In Nehemiah 3:13 we encounter "the Valley Gate." Could this not be used to represent the believer overcoming death (cf. Ps. 23:4)?

Now, of what use is "the Refuse Gate" (Neh. 3:13, 14)? Oh, but we find that this can represent hell, because Jesus, in Matthew 5:22, 29 and 30 spoke about *hell* using the analogy of manure being burned in a place called *Gehenna*, where they took the refuse outside of the city gates.

In Nehemiah 3:15 we see "the Fountain Gate." This could represent healing, because Jesus told a blind man, "Go, wash in the pool of Siloam" (John 9:7). And we find the result in John 9:11: "I went away and washed, and I received sight."

Nehemiah 3:26 tells of "the Water Gate." This must actually represent the Holy Spirit, we are told, because Jesus said in John 7:37:

> He who believes in Me, as the Scripture said, "From his innermost being will flow rivers of living water."

And John explains in verse 39:

> But this He spoke of the Spirit, whom those who believed in Him were to receive. . . .

"The Horse Gate" (Neh. 3:28) must surely be a reference to the power of the tongue, since James 3:3, 5 states:

> Now if we put the bits into the horses' mouths so that they will obey us, we direct their entire body as well. . . . So also the tongue is a small part of the body, and *yet* it boasts of great things.

So, when you see that horse gate, remember that you are supposed to control your tongue!

Finally, we arrive at "the East Gate" (Neh. 3:29). This, we are told, represents nothing less than the second coming of Christ Himself! That is because we read in Matthew 24:27:

> For just as the lightning comes from the east and flashes even to the west, so will the coming of the Son of Man be.

Alas, Nehemiah 3:31 takes us to "the Inspection Gate," which reminds us of the judgment seat of Christ. It is there that God is going to take our works and put them through a fire to *inspect* their quality.

This method of interpretation appears to give us a more spiritual understanding—a higher meaning—of the text. After all, who wants to hear a sermon about the city gates and wall, anyway? That is boring!

But what is the problem with all of this? Are not all of the meanings that are found in these gates true? Of course, they are—but the allegorist, in this case, is making a great sermon out of the wrong passage.

We hear much of this kind of preaching today. It contains many good ideas. It may even give you the liver quiver that you are looking for. But it leaves us asking: Where in the world is the allegorical interpreter or preacher getting this information? There is nothing in Nehemiah 3 about evangelism, conversion or controlling your tongue—to say nothing of the prophetic future!

Do you know what "the Fish Gate" really was? It was a place to transport fish. And it is the same with all these other gates.

You see, what really happened was that a mindset began to take control in Alexandria, moving the church into this realm of aggressive allegorization. They were no longer deriving their ideas from the text, but were rather reading them into the text. That is extremely dangerous.

This is the eclipse that eventually came over Antioch. This mentality is what eclipsed all that the church had taught for 200 years. And this mentality is what came to dominate the church for more than a thousand years. Ultimately, God raised up the Protestant Reformers to begin to correct this problem.

Irenaeus lived in the second century A.D., from roughly 125 to 202. There is a direct link between Irenaeus and the Apostle John: John discipled a man named Polycarp, and Polycarp discipled Irenaeus. Therefore, the beliefs of Irenaeus largely represent the beliefs of the apostles and the mindset of the school of Antioch, which dominated the early church for its first two centuries. Here is Bible scholar George N. H. Peters, introducing a statement from Irenaeus:

> The literal, grammatical interpretation of the Scriptures must . . . be observed in order to obtain a correct understanding. . . . The primitive church occupied this position, and Irenaeus . . . gives us the general sentiment . . . when he says of the Holy Scriptures: "that what the understanding can daily make use of, what it can easily know, is that which lies before our eyes, unambiguously, literally, and clearly in Holy Writ."[12]

Because these men had such a great respect for the Bible, they took

12 Quoted in George N. H. Peters, *The Theocratic Kingdom*, 3 vols. (New York: Funk & Wagnalls, 1884; reprint, Grand Rapids: Kregel, 1952), 1:47.

the whole Bible literally—including Bible prophecy. And that means, of course—among other things—that we are not currently living in the millennial kingdom! This literal interpretive method practiced at Antioch was eventually eclipsed by the allegorical method practiced at Alexandria.

Why should we not allegorize the Biblical text?

Dangers of Allegorization

More recently, J. Dwight Pentecost, in his classic textbook *Things to Come*, offered the major reasons why we should not utilize allegorical interpretation of the Bible.[13] I will summarize and expand upon them here as follows:

The Text is Not Being Interpreted

Instead of doing actual interpretation, you are bringing lots of ideas into the text which cannot actually be found there.

Pentecost here quotes Milton Terry, who wrote a classic book on hermeneutics—the science and art of Biblical interpretation. In it, he stated:

> ...it will be noticed at once that its habit is to disregard the common signification of words and give wing to all manner of fanciful speculation. It does not draw out the legitimate meaning of an author's language, but foists into it whatever the whim or fancy of an interpreter may desire.[14]

The allegorical interpreter may present some ideas that are spiritually true—but they do not naturally come from the text that he is basing them on. This is the difference between exegesis and eisegesis—drawing the meaning out of the text versus reading things into the passage that are not actually there. God is the authority, and I have no basis upon which to rewrite or edit God.

As has often been noted:

---

13 J. Dwight Pentecost, *Things to Come* (Grand Rapids: Zondervan, 1964), pp. 5-6.

14 Milton S. Terry, *Biblical Hermeneutics* (NY: Philips and Hunt, 1883), p. 224.

> Those who spiritualize tell spiritual lies, because they have no spiritual eyes.

When you are sitting under the ministry of an allegorist, you are under a perpetual liar.

The Interpreter Becomes the Authority over the Text

Allegorization places the importance on "the mind of the interpreter" (as Pentecost puts it), rather than on the Biblical text, where it belongs.

Again, Pentecost quotes Jerome, who was an allegorist himself, but made the following correct statement:

> ...once we start with the rule that whole passages and books of scripture say one thing when they mean another, the reader is delivered bound hand and foot to the caprice of the interpreter.[15]

There is No Way to Test the Interpreter

Allegorization is a highly subjective practice. One person can place one meaning on a text, while another may have a different interpretation. Which allegorist is correct?

There is no way to test which one is right, because once we start allegorizing we can come up with an endless variety of potential meanings for any given text.

There Is No Mechanism for Controlling the Interpreter's Imagination

Finally, we lose all control of the interpretation of the passage—leaving us to the whim of the sanctified imagination and the wild interpretations that it produces. And that sanctified imagination is really the evidence of a carnal mind.

---

15 Jerome, as quoted by F.W. Farrar, History of interpretation (NY: E.P. Dutton and Company, 1886), pp. 238-39.

Bernard Ramm, again quoted by Pentecost, put it this way:

> ...to state that the principal meaning of the Bible is a second-sense meaning, and that the principle method of interpretation is "spiritualizing," is to open the door to almost uncontrolled speculation and imagination. For this reason we have insisted that the control in interpretation is the literal method.[16]

I would add that what we must practice is *the literal method*—consistently applied. In other words, we must interpret Biblical words and phrases according to the ordinary sense that each one has. That, however, is a difficult practice that requires discipline and training. Yet we can do it if we are dedicated to the task. And it puts the Biblical text back in control over the speculation and imagination of the interpreter.

Reasons for the Shift to Allegorization

Why did the church discard literal interpretation and move into allegorization for 1,000 years? What caused this shift?

I would like to offer six factors that help to explain why this change happened.

The Need for Immediate Relevance

Once you move into allegorization, your teaching can immediately become relevant to the needs of the listener.

People do not want to think about the meaning of a passage—they want something that applies directly to their lives.

The preacher will often succumb to this pressure and finds that the fastest way to become relevant is to become allegorical.

As Dr. Howard Hendricks taught at Dallas Theological Seminary, the task of the preacher is to be both Biblical and relevant. The discipline of

16 Ramm, *Protestant Biblical Interpretation*, p. 65.

preaching and teaching is to establish meaning and bring it to people—but also to show them why it relates to their lives.

Ramm illustrates how allegorizing has the opposite effect when he states:

> But citing verses in the Old Testament, in themselves frequently very obscure, as if superior to verses in the New, revealed no understanding of the significance of historical and progressive revelation for hermeneutics. . . . They considered the Old (especially) and the New Testaments filled with parables, enigmas, and riddles. The allegorical method alone sufficed to bring out the meaning of these parables, enigmas, and riddles.[17]

The Incorporation of Human Philosophy into Interpretation

The Apostle Paul specifically warned against marrying Biblical interpretation with human philosophy, by stating:

> See to it that no one takes you captive through philosophy and empty deception, according to the tradition of men, according to the elementary principles of the world, rather than according to Christ. (Col. 2:8)

The full wisdom of Jesus Christ is limitless, but the teaching of man is *elementary*. This is like going back to kindergarten. It involves giving up the majesty and the depths of the wisdom of Christ. What a poor exchange this is! It is nothing less than giving up the thinking of God for the thinking of man.

The people at Alexandria became very philosophical. We can never merge the Bible with a human philosophy. They will never fit together, and the only way that we will be able to make them fit will be to allegorize the Bible. This can be true of the early chapters of Genesis—if you try to make it fit with the words of Darwin or the teaching of evolution. It can also be true if you attempt to make the Bible fit with the teachings of psychology.

17 Ibid., p. 30.

We can never allow human philosophy to displace spiritual truth.

The Influence of Gnostic Dualism

Alexandria was a hotbed of Gnosticism. One of their main teachings was dualism—that the physical world is bad but the spiritual world is good.

Is this Biblical? Notice, in fact, that God directly contracted this idea at the close of the sixth day of creation:

> God saw all that He had made, and behold, it was very good. And there was evening and there was morning, the sixth day. (Gen. 1:31)

The statement encompasses everything that God "had made," including all physical things. The physical world has since been marred by sin, but it is not inherently evil. But the Gnostics taught that it was. And once that becomes your philosophy, it begins to wreak havoc on other Biblical doctrines—and it destroys Christology, in particular.

You see, the Gnostics did not understand how Jesus could have come in a human body since the physical world—in their thinking—is evil. This led to the development of Cerinthianism, based on the heretic Cerinthus, who taught that Jesus was not born as the Christ, but rather that the spirit of Christ came upon Him at His baptism. Cerinthus also said that the spirit of Christ left Jesus before He died.

When you understand these teachings, you understand the background of the book of 1 John and the reasons why the Apostle John makes statements like this which are aimed directly at Cerinthus:

> Who is the liar but the one who denies that Jesus is the Christ? This is the antichrist, the one who denies the Father and the Son. (1 John 2:22)

Gnostic dualism also took the form of docetism, which is from a Greek word meaning *to seem* or *to appear*. Docetists taught that Jesus did not actually have a body—that He only appeared to have a body. This again is answered by the Apostle John:

> By this you know the Spirit of God: every spirit that confesses that Jesus Christ has come in the flesh is from God; and every spirit that does not confess Jesus is not from God; this is the *spirit* of the antichrist, of which you have heard that it is coming, and now it is already in the world. (1 John 4:2-3)

These kinds of teachings were very prominent in the Mediterranean world. Thus, when Paul spoke to the pagan Greek philosophers on Mars Hill, he faced this reaction:

> Now when they heard of the resurrection of the dead, some *began* to sneer, but others said, "We shall hear you again concerning this." (Acts 17:32)

This mindset also migrated over to neighboring Corinth, so Paul also had to write to that church, stating:

> Now if Christ is preached, that He has been raised from the dead, how do some among you say that there is no resurrection of the dead? (1 Cor. 15:12)

Now, remember, the Christians in Antioch believed in a future, earthly kingdom of Christ. But in Alexandria they began to deny this reality. After all, they reasoned, how can there be a physical kingdom one day here in this world when we know that the physical world is evil? This led to the development of the doctrine of amillennialism, and the teaching that we are living in the kingdom right now in spiritual form only.

But what about all the detailed prophecies of the future kingdom? These have to be allegorized, of course, to fit into the amillennial system.

Taken literally, these prophecies indicate that the kingdom will be physical, and it will even involve eating and drinking, according to Jesus:

> I say to you that many will come from east and west, and recline *at the table* with Abraham, Isaac and Jacob in the kingdom of heaven. (Matt. 8:11)
>
> And they will come from east and west and from north and south, and will recline *at the table* in the kingdom of God. (Luke 13:29)
>
> But I say to you, I will not drink of this fruit of the vine from now on until that day when I drink it new with you in My Father's kingdom. (Matt. 26:29)

But the people in Alexandria did not see how this could be. How could there be a physical kingdom if the physical world is evil?

Writing about Augustine, who was pivotal in this change of thinking that swept through the church, Dr. Renald Showers writes:

> The . . . factor in his change of view was the influence of Greek philosophy upon his thinking. Before his conversion Augustine was deeply immersed in the study of this philosophy, much of which asserted the inherent evil of the physical or material and the inherent goodness of the totally spiritual. This philosophy continued to leave its mark upon him even after his conversion. It prompted him to reject as carnal the pre-millennial idea of an earthly, political Kingdom of God with great material blessings. He believed that, in order for the Kingdom of God to be good, it must be spiritual in nature.[18]

Here is something that we may learn from Augustine's experience: When a person is saved, especially later in life, he or she will inevitably drag the old ways of thinking into the Christian life. This is why our minds must be renewed as directed in Scripture (Rom. 12:2).

18 Renald Showers and John Ankerberg, *The Most Asked Prophecy Questions* (Chattanooga, TN: ATRI, 2000), p. 326.

Augustine was a brilliant man, but he never went through that change. Thus, he thought that in order for the kingdom to be good, it must be non-physical. This leads to this terrible doctrine of amillennialism.

In fact, Augustine gave us the very first formal treatment of amillennialism in the fourth century—his famous work, *The City of God*. Notice what he said:

> And this opinion would not be objectionable, if it were believed that the joys of the saints in that Sabbath shall be spiritual, and consequent on the presence of God; for I myself, too, once held this opinion. But, as they assert that those who then rise again shall enjoy the leisure of immoderate carnal banquets, furnished with an amount of meat and drink such as not only to shock the feeling of the temperate, but even to surpass the measure of credulity itself, such assertions can be believed only by the carnal. They who do believe them are called by the spiritual Chiliasts, which we may literally reproduce by the name Millenarians.[19]

You see, in Augustine's mind, Gnostic dualism won out over the clear teachings of the Bible.

Yet the Apostle Paul thought differently, as explained in this verse:

> For everything created by God is good, and nothing is to be rejected if it is received with gratitude; for it is sanctified by means of the word of God and prayer. (1 Tim. 4:4-5)

The Decline of the Church's Jewish Population

Remember, there were no Gentile believers in the church until the conversion of Cornelius in Acts 10. By the time Paul launches his missionary journeys from Antioch, we begin to see a pattern. Everywhere he went, the Jews, with very few exceptions, rejected the gospel—while the Gentiles

19 Augustine, *The City of God*, trans., Marcus Dods (NY: Random House, 1950), Book XX, chap. 7, p. 719.

embraced it. Notice what happened in Southern Galatia on Paul's first missionary journey:

> But when the Jews saw the crowds, they were filled with jealousy and *began* contradicting the things spoken by Paul, and were blaspheming. (Acts 13:45)

By contrast,

> When the Gentiles heard this, they *began* rejoicing and glorifying the word of the Lord; and as many as had been appointed to eternal life believed. (Acts 13:48)

Similar things happened almost everywhere Paul went. And, as a result, the ethnic population of the church began to change—from being almost all Jewish to being almost all Gentile.

In fact, this problem becomes so acute that Paul must warn the Gentiles, stating:

> But I am speaking to you who are Gentiles. Inasmuch then as I am an apostle of Gentiles, I magnify my ministry. … But if some of the branches were broken off, and you, being a wild olive, were grafted in among them and became partaker with them of the rich root of the olive tree, do not be arrogant toward the branches; but if you are arrogant, *remember that* it is not you who supports the root, but the root *supports* you. You will say then, "Branches were broken off so that I might be grafted in." Quite right, they were broken off for their unbelief, but you stand by your faith. Do not be conceited, but fear; for if God did not spare the natural branches, He will not spare you, either. (Rom. 11:13, 17-21)

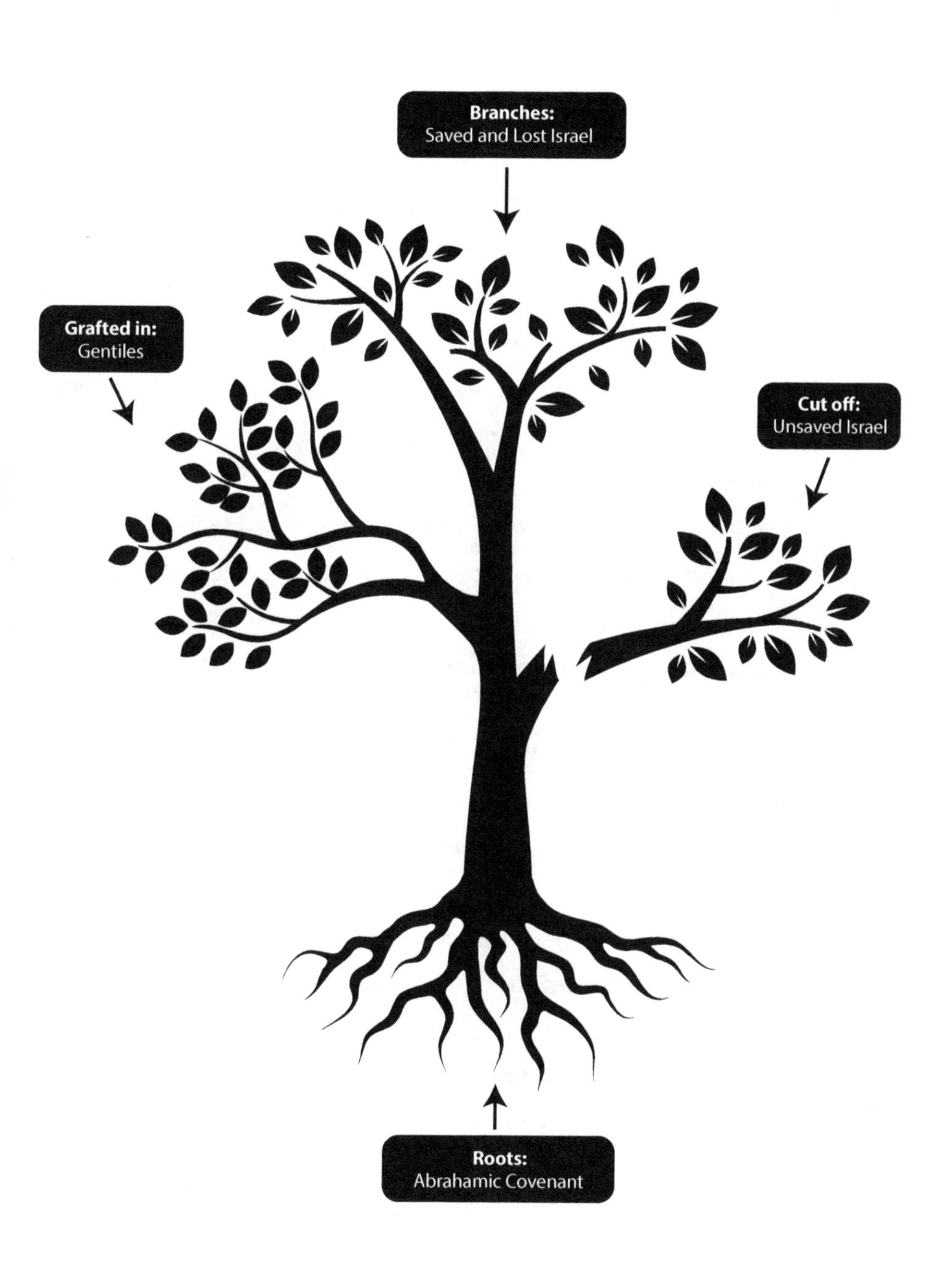
Branches:
Saved and Lost Israel
Grafted in:
Gentiles
Cut off:
Unsaved Israel
Roots:
Abrahamic Covenant

Paul is telling the Romans that if God has the power to take *wild*, unnatural branches and graft them into this olive tree of blessing, then it certainly would not be difficult for Him to place natural branches back into their own tree.

In fact, following the rapture of the church, that is exactly what God is going to do. Therefore, Gentiles believers have no basis for being arrogant—especially toward the Jews.

Now here is the point: Alexandrian and Augustinian thinking would never have taken over the church if the composition of the church had remained Jewish. That is because Jews are steeped in the Old Testament from birth, and they interpret it literally. They would never have accepted the doctrine of amillennialism.

But Gentiles did not know the Old Testament or Hebrew, and they accepted these false allegorical teachings quickly through the early centuries of the church.

There is another factor involved in this shift.

Constantine's Edict of Milan (313 A.D.)

Constantine, the Roman emperor, ended the formal Roman persecution of Christians and gave Christianity a recognized status within the empire in 313 A.D.

Christians had been persecuted by Rome since 64 A.D., in the days of Nero. They had been thrown to the lions in the coliseum or set on fire to illuminate garden parties. Constantine not only ended such persecution, but began to elevate and promote Christianity.

If you were a Christian living through that transition, what would you have thought? Surely it would be logical to think that the kingdom had come, and that Revelation 20 was being fulfilled when it says:

> They will be priests of God and of Christ and will reign with Him for a thousand years. (Rev. 20:6)

You see, the politics of the day allowed for allegorization and amillennialism to take off like a rocket. In fact, the church went under an allegorical spell that lasted for more than 1,000 years.

Showers describes it this way:

> That new view became known as Amillennialism. Several things prompted this change in Augustine. First, the political situation of the Church in the Roman empire had changed radically around the period of his life. By his time the Roman persecution of the Church had stopped, and the state had made itself the servant of the Church. As the Roman empire crumbled, the Church stood fast, ready to rule in the place of the empire. It looked as if Gentile world dominion was being crushed and that the Church was becoming victorious over it. Under these circumstances Augustine concluded that Premillennialism was obsolete, and that it did not fit the current situation. In the place of it he developed the idea that the Church is the Kingdom of the Messiah foretold in such Scriptures as Daniel 2 and 7 and Revelation 20. In his book, *The City of God*, he became the first person to teach the idea that the organized Catholic (Universal) Church is the promised Messianic Kingdom and that the Millennium began with the first coming of Christ.[20]

Prior to Constantine, Augustine's ideas would not have taken a foothold. But with this shift in place, they became very palatable.

There is one final factor to consider.

The Events of 70 A.D. and Hadrian's Palestine

In 70 A.D., the Romans came and pushed the Jews out of the land of Israel, burning and destroying the temple brick-by-brick.

Christ had predicted this as discipline for the nation for its rejection of Him as king (cf. Matt. 24:2). The Jews went into worldwide dispersion, and did not return to the land until 1948.

20 Renald Showers, *The Most Asked Prophecy Questions*, p. 325.

As long as there were Jews in Israel worshiping in the temple, it appeared as though the Old Testament prophecies about them should be taken literally. But after 70 A.D., there were no Jews in the land. That created the right intellectual climate in which people would question the literal interpretation of the Scripture related to the nation of Israel. After all, Israel did not even exist anymore!

The Roman emperor Hadrian, who ruled from 117 to 138 A.D., went into Israel and renamed it *Palestine*. He was trying to de-Judaize the land. He wanted to act as if the Jews were never even in that land at all and had no historical claim to it. He picked the name *Palestine*, which is a linguistic derivation from the name *Philistine*—representing ancient enemies of the land of Israel. He was trying to mock and humiliate the Jewish people and revise history.

The Bible never uses the term Palestine, and we should not either. It is essentially an anti-Jewish slur, as intended by Hadrian. We should use the proper Biblical designation for that land, as recorded in Matthew 2:21:

> So Joseph got up, took the Child and His mother, and came into *the land of Israel.* (italics added)

But after 70 A.D., the Jewish claims to the land were basically erased. In fact, unless you were a Bible reader, you might not even know that the Jewish people once lived there.

In sum, the preceding discussion indicates that for six reasons Alexandrian allegorization won the day over Antioch's literalism. They include: the desire for immediate relevance in Bible interpretation, the incorporation of human philosophy into Bible interpretation, the influence of gnostic dualism, the church's growing gentile population, Constantine's Edict of Milan, and the events of 70 A D.

Two Key Allegorists

You cannot understand and appreciate what God did through the Reformers when He used them to pull the church back toward Biblical truth until you first understand what the devil did to influence people away from the truth and destroy the church's Biblical teaching.

Two major allegorists in particular came out of the school at Alexandria and exercised a huge influence over the thinking of the church for thousands of years.

The first was Origen, who lived from 185 to 254 A.D. Diprose states regarding Origen:

> Origen was also influenced by the example of Philo, a first-century Alexandrian Jew who had interpreted the Old Testament Scriptures allegorically in order to make them harmonize with his Platonism. Allegorism played an important part in Origen's theory of interpretation and, as he was the first biblical scholar to work out 'a complete hermeneutical theory', his work was destined to exert great influence on the Christian approach to the Hebrew Scriptures, for centuries to come. . . . Origen is remembered for his philosophical speculation as the allegorist *par excellence* among Biblical interpreters.[21]

In other words, Origen took the ideas of Philo, brought them into Christian thought and began to develop them further intellectually.

To be fair, Origen did contribute other things, such as the *Hexapla*, that are very helpful to Christian thought. Sometimes people have a tendency to think that if someone did one good thing, then everything they did must be good. But that is not always the case.

As we have already seen, Augustine (354—430 A.D.)—the second key interpreter—is the most influential theologian in church history. He has exerted more influence over how Christians have thought over the last 2,000

21 Diprose, *Israel in the Development of Christian Thought*, pp. 86-87.

years than any other single figure. While he also did do some good things, his influence was certainly not all used for good. After he gave the church its first formal treatise on amillennialism, *The City of God* (probably the most influential Christian book that has ever been written), amillennialism and allegorization took off. And that led to the Dark Ages.

Origen gave Augustine the hermeneutic. Augustine developed and applied that hermeneutic further, especially to the area of eschatology.

For instance, Ezekiel 47:8 talks about the Dead Sea coming back to life biologically. To the allegorist, a prophecy such as this would be taken to speak of the unbeliever becoming a believer and receiving new life. That interpretation also has the advantage of being interesting and relevant!

One very important passage that Augustine wrote about is Revelation 20:1-4:

> Then I saw an angel coming down from heaven, holding the key of the abyss and a great chain in his hand. And he laid hold of the dragon, the serpent of old, who is the devil and Satan, and bound him for a thousand years; and he threw him into the abyss, and shut *it* and sealed *it* over him, so that he would not deceive the nations any longer, until the thousand years were completed; after these things he must be released for a short time.
>
> Then I saw thrones, and they sat on them, and judgment was given to them. And I *saw* the souls of those who had been beheaded because of their testimony of Jesus and because of the word of God, and those who had not worshiped the beast or his image, and had not received the mark on their forehead and on their hand; and they came to life and reigned with Christ for a thousand years.

But Augustine thought that Satan was already bound, and taught that this "first resurrection" (Rev. 20:5) to life here is regeneration. He taught that the church is the reigning kingdom of God upon the Earth right now. This paved the way for the beginning of Roman Catholicism's doctrine that the Roman Catholic Church now represents kingdom of God on Earth.

Here is what he wrote about it:

> The saints reign with Christ during the same thousand years, understood in the same way, that is, of the time of His first coming. . . .
>
> Therefore the Church even now is the kingdom of Christ, and the kingdom of heaven. Accordingly, even now His saints reign with Him.[22]

But Paul tells us that Satan is "the god of this world" (2 Cor. 4:4). And "the first resurrection" (of two resurrections) is the physical resurrection of tribulation martyrs and Old Testament saints who will rule with Christ under His delegated authority—for 1,000 years. Unbelievers will be raised to damnation following that time. Sadly, Augustine's misunderstanding is a problem that the Protestant Reformers never corrected.

Decline of Chiliasm

Through the influence of Augustine, chiliasm and the literal interpretation of Bible prophecy began to be viewed as a relic of the past—something for the less enlightened.

Eusebius (260—340 A.D.), the well-known church historian and author of *Ecclesiastical History*, wrote about the literalist and chiliast, Papias (60—130 A.D.), stating:

> Papias . . . says that there will be a millennium after the resurrections of the dead, when the kingdom of Christ will be set up in material form on this earth. I suppose that he got these notions by *a perverse reading of the apostolic accounts, not realizing that they had spoken mystically and symbolically. For he was a man of very*

22 Augustine, *The City of God*, Book XX, chap. 9, pp. 725-26.

> *little intelligence, as is clear from his books*. But he is responsible for the fact that so many Christian writers after him held the same opinion, relying on his antiquity, for instance Irenaeus and whoever else appears to have held the same views.[23] (italics added)

Tertullian, quoting Jerome (347—420 A.D.), who was heavily influenced by Augustinian thought, wrote:

> How must we understand what the Saviour says in Matthew: 'But I say to you, I will not drink again of this fruit of the vine until that day when I drink it new with you in the Kingdom of my Father'? (Matth. 26. 29). This passage is the origin of *a certain fable of a thousand years*, in which they say that Christ will reign in the flesh and will drink that wine which He has not drunk since that time until the end of the world.... For the kingdom of God isn't food and drink, but justice, joy and peace in the Holy Spirit (Rom. 14. 17).[24] (italics added)

Jerome was quoting Romans 14:17 incorrectly. And he was showing how far the church had moved since the days of Antioch.

This chapter has surveyed how the allegorical interpretive practice of Alexandria, Egypt eventually supplanted the literal interpretive practice of Syrian Antioch. This interpretive shift plummeted the church into a period of time known as the *Dark Ages*, which will be described in the next chapter. The Protestant Reformers, by contrast, sought to take the church back to Antioch, and to recover much that had been lost since that time. How well did they do this? We will find out in the ensuing chapters.

23 Eusebius, *Ecclesiastical History*, 3.39.12-13.

24 Jerome, "Letter 120 (Ad Hedibiam). To Hedibia, on biblical problems (Excerpts)," http://www.tertullian.org/fathers/jerome_letter_120.htm; Internet; accessed 10 June 2017.

CHAPTER 3

The Dark Ages

The Dark Ages, or the Middle Ages, lasted from the fourth century A.D.—roughly the time of Augustine—all the way to the 16th century. This is why God began to touch the hearts of the Protestant Reformers, because He loves His church.

The Protestant Reformation was a rescue operation to take the church back from a mindset that had reigned in Christendom for more than 1,000 years—longer than the millennial kingdom will be!

Dark Ages Timeline

A. Lasted from the 4th to the 16th centuries

B. Obsolescence of prophetic studies

C. Domination of Augustinian Amillennialism

D. Only one church: Roman Catholicism

E. The Bible is removed from the people

1. Allegorization
2. Illiteracy
3. Mass read in Latin

F. Sale of indulgences

G. Anti-Semitism

H. Church in need of rescue

The Dominance of Kingdom Now Theology

The study of prophecy became totally obsolete during this time. What dominated instead was Augustinian amillennialism.

Showers states:

> Augustine's allegorical amillennialism became the official doctrine of the church, and Premillennialism went underground. Some aspects of Premillennialism were even branded as heretical. The Roman Catholic Church strongly advocated and maintained Augustine's Amillennial view throughout the Middle Ages. During that span of time occasionally premillennial groups formed to challenge the doctrine and political power of the major part of organized Christendom, but they were not able to restore Premillennialism to its original position as the accepted, orthodox view of the Church.[25]

As Showers states, there were a few premillennial groups here and there during these centuries, but they were not the norm. How far the church had moved since the days of Justin Martyr, when he said that unless you believed in chiliasm (premillennialism)—the prophecies that there will be a future, literal kingdom upon the Earth—you are not an orthodox Christian. That is what the church had believed for 200 years, but now it had almost disappeared from Christian thought.

But God always has a remnant in every generation (cf. 1 Kings 19:18). Jesus promised in Matthew 16:18:

---

25 Renald Showers and John Ankerberg, *The Most Asked Prophecy Questions* (Chattanooga, TN: ATRI, 2000), pp. 327-28.

> I also say to you that you are Peter, and upon this rock I will build My church; and the gates of Hades will not overpower it.

You can even look back during the Dark Ages and find people, like little blips of light on the radar screen, who stood for the truth—but they were few and far in between. They did not have positions of influence, and did not represent organized Christendom.

One such man, named Pseudo Ephraem, lived sometime during the fourth through sixth centuries A.D. He was a Syrian who was possibly using the pen name *Ephraem* in order to escape persecution. He may not have been the famous Ephraem the Syriac. But this quotation of him was discovered on a fragment from his day:

> Why therefore do we not reject every care of earthly actions and prepare ourselves for the meeting of the Lord Christ, so that he may draw us from the confusion, which overwhelms all the world. . . . For all the saints and the elect of god are gathered, prior to the tribulation that is to come, and are taken to the Lord lest they see the confusion that is to overwhelm the world because of our sins.[26]

This sounds very much like the basis for understanding a literal tribulation period, preceded by a literal rapture of the church. Here was a man who was reading the Bible and taking it literally—regardless of what everyone else in Christendom thought!

Yes, there was always a believing remnant, but these people never represented a reigning sentiment for the truth, which had reigned originally for two centuries thanks to the influence of Antioch.

---

26 Timothy J. Demy and Thomas D. Ice, "The Rapture and an Early Medieval Citation," *Bibliotheca Sacra* 152, no. 607 (July-September 1995): 305-16.

The Removal of the Scriptures from the Laity

Remember also that during these days there was only one church to attend—the Roman Catholic Church. It had bought completely into Augustinian allegorization, which had the effect of removing the Bible from the people.

You see, the Bible was not at all accessible. It had not even been translated into the people's language! More than that, in cathedrals all over Europe, it was literally chained to the pulpit. Average people were told that they could not understand the Bible for themselves. The priests proudly proclaimed that they were the only ones who had the formal training to exercise the allegorical interpretation of the day. The Bible was thus given to the people through the lens of the elevated priesthood. The lay people were neither expected nor even allowed to read it on their own.

This, in turn, made the people gullible for manipulation by the priests. After all, if the priest had the only Bible in the church, and told the people that he was the only one who could understand it, then he could get those people to do anything that he wanted them to do—including works to get their relatives out of purgatory.

The priests displayed their newfound power by dressing in fancy and colorful robes modeled after Aaron the high priest (cf. Ex. 28:2). There is nothing of this in the New Testament, so their authority came from the Old Testament—believing that the church had replaced the nation of Israel.

The New Testament, on the other hand, stresses the priesthood of all believers:

> He has made us *to be* a kingdom, priests to His God and Father—to Him *be* the glory and the dominion forever and ever. Amen. (Rev. 1:6)

We take the Bible for granted today, but these people did not even own

Bibles. Yet even if they had owned them, they could not have read them! They were not literate. There was no emphasis on public education such as we have, or any such thing. We will see later how the Reformers worked to overcome these shortcomings of the Dark Ages.

Sometimes I chuckle when people tell me that the particular views of Bible prophecy to which I hold have not been taught in the church for 1,800 years. Yet people were illiterate for much of this time period! Furthermore, they had no Bibles to read! Should the Dark Ages be the standard of correct doctrine? Beliefs that were lost after the fourth century A.D. and not fully discovered until the last few centuries, therefore, are not necessarily illegitimate.

The priests were further empowered—and exalted among the lay people—through the use of Latin for the Mass.

In the fourth century A.D., Jerome had set out to translate the Bible from Hebrew and Greek into Latin, the *lingua franca* of the Roman Empire. The problem was that it had become a dead language.

The Roman Catholic Church kept using it, however, with no thought for the impact this would have upon the common people. The average person would not even understand what was being said in church! It reminds us of the abuse of the gift of tongues in 1 Corinthians 14. The point was that there was nothing edifying about someone babbling in a tongue that was not understood. It would have no educational value at all. So, the situation required an interpreter:

> If anyone speaks in a tongue, *it should be* by two or at the most three, and *each* in turn, and one must interpret; but if there is no interpreter, he must keep silent in the church; and let him speak to himself and to God. (1 Cor. 14:27-28)

A church service or Mass being conducted in Latin, likewise, has no ability to edify listeners who do not understand Latin. At most, they would be able to observe things like stained glass windows and have an emotional experience.

The Sale of Indulgences

Tragically, this led to the sale of indulgences within the church. The unwary had no defense against this practice. It was based on the unbiblical doctrine of purgatory, which was used to play upon people's emotions. In fact, they even had a saying about it that rhymed:

> When the coin in the coffer rings,
> the soul from purgatory springs.

The sale of indulgences became a huge money-making operation, because most rational people would like to get their relatives out of purgatory. It was personified by a friar named Johann Tetzel. His manipulation of the people truly upset Luther.

Imagine how you feel when you see your Christian beliefs prostituted for the sake of raising money by false teachers on religious television. This makes you feel a sense of righteous indignation, does it not?

Multiply that emotion by 100—or even 1,000—and you know how Martin Luther felt when he saw people that he loved being manipulated by the priests.

Tetzel used this version of the rhyme to sell indulgences:

> As soon as the gold in the casket rings;
> the rescued soul to heaven springs.

Yet his sermons terrorized the common people. Here is just one statement that he made—appealing to the listeners' obligations to deceased relatives:

> Don't you hear the voices of your wailing dead parents and oth-

> ers who say, "Have mercy upon me, have mercy upon me, because we are in severe punishment and pain. From this you could redeem us with a small alms and yet you do not want to do so." Open your ears as the father says to the son and the mother to the daughter, "We have created you, fed you, cared for you, and left you our temporal goods. Why then are you so cruel and harsh that you do not want to save us, though it only takes a little? You let us lie in flames so that we only slowly come to the promised glory."

Tetzel even promised the people "complete remission of all their sins" and "full remission of the punishment which belongs to sin" if they would just "put alms into the coffer."[27]

You can see how this would terrorize people! They were set up for total manipulation.

We know how God feels about the corruption of His Word for money. Jesus, in fact, went into the temple on two different occasions—once at the beginning of His ministry and once at the end of His ministry—and became so angry that He "overturned their tables" (John 2:15). Why did He do this? Because, they had turned His "Father's house" (John 2:16) into a marketplace.

The Solomonic Temple was supposed to bring the knowledge of God—and show the glory of God—to the people of all nations who visited it, like the Queen of Sheba (1 Kings 10:1-10). But now it was nothing more than a money-making operation, and Jesus became incensed at that, because that which had been given to attract the nations to God became something that repulsed the nations.

Luther experienced something similar, but his ecclesiastical superiors looked the other way, because the gravy train was rolling in. This much-needed money was necessary to build St. Peter's Basilica in Rome. That was

27 For the entirely of Tetzel's sermon, see "Preaching Future Security – Johann Tetzel, *Sermon on Indulgences* (c. 1517)," http://germanhistorydocs.ghi-dc.org/sub_document.cfm?document_id=4207; Internet; accessed 1 November 2017.

an expensive proposition!

The civil governors were also very happy with the indulgences, because they received some of this money, as well.

The Inability to Test All Things

The people of the church, however, had no ability to "examine everything *carefully*" and then to "hold fast to that which is good" (1 Thess. 5:21), because they had no Bibles.

We underestimate what a great gift the Bible is to us—not only the fact that we have it and can access it, but also that we can also understand it, and thus be able to discern truth from error. It is part of our defensive armor (cf. Eph. 6:17), and it is able to support us in times of temptation (cf. Matt. 4:4, 7, 10).

During the Dark Ages, the capacity to be a Berean was lost. What is a Berean? It is someone who models his or her behavior after the believers at Berea on Paul's second missionary journey in the book of Acts:

> The brethren immediately sent Paul and Silas away by night to Berea, and when they arrived, they went into the synagogue of the Jews. Now these were more noble-minded than those in Thessalonica, for they received the word with great eagerness, examining the Scriptures daily *to see* whether these things were so. (Acts 17:10-11)

Notice that the Bereans were first of all teachable, but that they did not receive any teaching uncritically. They measured all things by the Old Testament Scriptures that they had, for they knew that God does not lie, and thus everything that Paul taught them must be consistent with the Old Testament and not contradict it. They screened everything that Paul said against the Bibles that they possessed. They were given to the daily study of the written Word of God. And, keep in mind, they were scrutinizing God's chief apostle in this way! How much more should we be doing this daily with everything that we hear. And how much more can we who have the complete canon of the New Testament in our possession do it effectively today.

Even the carnal Corinthians were exhorted to practice discernment when listening to the active prophets of their day:

> Let two or three prophets speak, and let the others pass judgment. (1 Cor. 14:29)

The only way to *pass judgment* is through the record of God's revealed truth.

You see, the devil can give us many different kinds of experiences—including visions, signs and wonders. Two major false religions—Islam and Mormonism—began when someone (Muhammad and Joseph Smith, respectively) had contact with "an angel of light" (2 Cor. 11:14). Doubtless, these angels appeared to be very real to these men. The problem is that they assumed that the communications were from God. Of course, they could not have been from God in either case, because the messages contradict the Bible. So they had to be from the devil, who has a great deal of authority in the world today. If you are not actively testing all that you hear against that which God has revealed in His Word, you will inevitably fall into false teaching. Yet, today, many people assign truth based on their experiences. But experience is not the test of truth.

Christ commended the church at Ephesus, saying:

> I know your deeds and your toil and perseverance, and that you cannot tolerate evil men, and you put to the test those who call themselves apostles, and they are not, and you found them *to be* false. (Rev. 2:2)

This is a practice that is being lost in the 21st century.

Do you know how bankers learn to sense that they are in contact with counterfeit money? It is by studying the real thing. They become familiar with its appearance, color, texture and feel. This allows them to detect the presence of the counterfeit. They have a standard against which to compare it.

There is literally an explosion of false teaching in our world today—to the point that there is no way that it is possible to keep up with all of it. In fact, it would require an entire lifetime to become an expert in just one area of false teaching.

God is not calling all of us to understand every area of false teaching. What He is calling us to understand is His Word—a finite amount of revealed information.

The better you understand the 66 books of the Bible, the more easily you will recognize false teaching when it crosses your path.

In the Middle Ages, people had no such ability, as they did not have access to the truth.

Unrestrained Anti-Semitism

This time in history was also marked by anti-Semitism—rampant Jew hatred. In the previous chapter we learned some of the reasons for the development of this trend during the Middle Ages, and we have a record of anti-Semitism from the first century in the book of Acts. Acts 18:1-2 describes Paul's experience at Corinth:

> After these things he left Athens and went to Corinth. And he found a Jew named Aquila, a native of Pontus, having recently come from Italy with his wife Priscilla, because *Claudius had commanded all the Jews to leave Rome*. (italics added)

Satan hates the Jewish people. For one reason, he knows that the kingdom is going to come to the Earth through the Jewish people. His strategy throughout history has been to exterminate them. Thus, the normal mode of thought in the world is anti-Semitism. The only one who has a defense against that is the Bible reader and believer who believes in Scripture's declaration concerning national Israel's future.

One of the church's biggest black eyes comes from the poor manner in which many Christians have viewed and treated the Jewish people. Throughout the Middle Ages, anti-Semitism was widespread within the professing church. It was a church in need of rescue.

God's Faithfulness to His Church

We began this chapter by looking at Matthew 16:18:

> I also say to you that you are Peter, and upon this rock I will build My church; and the gates of Hades will not overpower it.

Jesus here calls Peter *little stone*, a masculine noun, but says he will build the church on a *big rock*, a neuter noun. Keep this clearly in mind, as we will revisit this concept in future chapters. Note that Jesus is not proclaiming Peter to be the first pope. In fact, He calls him "Satan" just a few verses later in Matthew 16:23. In addition, we know that Peter was married, as well (cf. Matt. 8:14-15), which would seemingly disqualify him from being labeled as the first pope.

But the main point here is that the *rock* is not Peter—but rather his declaration of Jesus as Messiah and God (Matt. 16:13-16). Christ would build His church on this statement of faith. Because of Christ's promise that His church would not be overtaken by Satan, it was just a matter of time before God worked within history in order to rescue His church from the dangers that overwhelmed her during the Dark Ages. As we will see in the next chapter, God began to accomplish this monumental feat through the work of the Protestant Reformers.

The Dark Ages Return

Sadly, to a large extent, Christendom (we might even say *Evangelicalism*) is moving back into the Dark Ages. Almost everywhere you turn in the writings of the emergent church, or emerging church, there is a perpetual denigration of the things that Martin Luther believed, in terms of Bible literacy and Bible teaching.

For instance, Doug Pagitt states:

> At Solomon's porch, sermons are not primarily about my extracting truth from the Bible to apply to people's lives. . . . So our sermons are not lessons that precisely define belief so much as they are stories that welcome our hopes and ideas and participation.[28]

This statement is in opposition to all that we should be attempting to do in ministry today. Our goal is to explain the truth of the Bible and apply it to people's lives. If you put your ear to the ground, you will hear Martin Luther rolling over in his grave at such talk.

Dan Kimball goes further:

> It isn't about clever apologetics or careful exegetical or expository preaching. . . . Emerging generations are hungering to experience God in worship.[29]

But that defies everything that John Calvin was about. He wrote detailed commentaries on almost every Biblical book. His life revolved around the careful exegetical and expository teaching of Scripture.

Again, Leonard Sweet goes even further:

> A spiritual Tsunami has hit postmodern culture. The wave will

28 Doug Pagitt, cited in Roger Oakland, *Faith Undone: The Emerging Church...A New Reformation or an End-Time Deception* (Silverton, OR: Lighthouse Trails, 2007), pp. 41-42.

29 Dan Kimball, cited in Oakland, *Faith Undone*, p. 58.

> build without breaking for decades to come. The wave is this: People want to *know* God. They want less to know about God ... they want new experiences, especially new experiences of the divine.[30]

Now, knowing God personally is an admirable goal. But how do you do that without studying how He has revealed Himself in His Word?

It seems like everywhere we turn today there is someone shooting at the idea of careful Bible exposition.

Brian McLaren stated,

> . . . something beyond a belief system or doctrinal array or even a practice. I mean an attitude—an attitude toward God and our neighbor and our mission that is *passionate*.[31]

Passion is a good thing, but how do you know you are worshiping the right Jesus? The only way that you can ever know that is through doctrine.

We need proper behavior, but we must first anchor it in proper beliefs.

Rick Warren has made a number of similar statements in his very popular book, *The Purpose Driven Life*:

> God won't ask you about your religious background or doctrinal views.[32]
>
> Jesus said our love for each other—not our doctrinal beliefs—is our greatest witness to the world.[33]
>
> Today many assume that spiritual maturity is measured by the amount of biblical information and doctrine you know.[34]
>
> The Bible is far more than a doctrinal guidebook.[35]

---

30 Leonard Sweet, cited in Oakland, *Faith Undone*, p. 54.

31 Brian McLaren, *A Generous Orthodoxy* (Grand Rapids: Zondervan, 2004), pp. 117-18.

32 Rick Warren, *The Purpose Driven Life* (Grand Rapids: Zondervan, 2002), 34.

33 Ibid., 124.

34 Ibid., 183.

35 Ibid., 186.

> The last thing many believers need today is to go to another Bible study. They already know far more than they are putting into practice.[36]

All of these statements disparage the careful preaching and teaching of doctrine. But what you believe about doctrine actually determines if you will even go to heaven! If we do not understand the sacrificial death of Christ in our place, we have no framework for loving other people at all, anyway.

The Biblical priority of preaching is evident in both testaments in passages such as 2 Kings 22; Nehemiah 8; Matthew 4:4; Acts 2:42; and 2 Timothy 3:15–4:2. There is a huge priority placed on Bible study and teaching.

In the Old Testament, there are times of brightness when God brings forth a revival. But every authentic revival in the Old Testament is precipitated by a return to the Scripture and careful Bible teaching. You cannot have true revival without the Word of God.

Dan Wallace correctly states regarding just the book of Second Timothy:

> By my count, there are twenty-seven explicit commands given in the body of this letter. In 27 words Paul tells pastors what to focus on. You have to be blind to miss the thrust of Paul's instructions here, because eighteen of those commands—fully two-thirds—have to do with the ministry of the Word.[37]

Yet the emergent church is moving away from all of that. One writer shared:

> Post-moderns prefer to encounter Christ by using all their senses. That's part of the appeal of classical liturgical or contemplative worship: the incense and candles, making the sign of the

36 Ibid., 231.

37 Daniel Wallace, "Crisis of the Word: A Message to Pastors or Would-be Pastors," *Conservative Theological Journal* 1, no. 2 (August 1997): 108.

> cross, the taste and smell of the bread and wine, touching icons and being anointed with oil.[38]

I grew up in this type of church—with the smells and the bells. And I was unregenerate. There is nothing magical in any of these things. The only thing that can change anyone is the Word of God and the gospel.

Kimball shares more of his view of preaching:

> . . . multisensory and interactive. . . . Through various experimental elements as well as through the space itself, we can actually preach. Art preaches. Scripture preaches. Music preaches. Even silence preaches.[39]

We see again here the de-emphasizing of the exposition of the Scriptures. And if this message is all new to you, be assured that it is not new to your children or grandchildren. They are hearing it wherever they turn. We must become equipped to reach the next generation, who are influenced by this type of teaching.

Notice where McLaren wants to take the church:

> If Charismatics gave me my high school diploma in the ways of the Spirit, it was from Catholic contemplatives that I entered an undergraduate degree in the liberal arts of the Spirit.[40]

McLaren wants to go back and retrieve ideas from the pre-Reformation Catholic Church and inject them anew into the life of the church today. This would include things like the stations of the cross, holy water, monasticism (now called *spiritual formation*) and labyrinths. This is nothing less than returning to the Dark Ages, from which the Reformers rescued us.

The emergent church tells us that we must get back to these ancient practices, which were utilized during the Dark Ages and then lost. But what

38 Julie B. Sevig, cited in Oakland, *Faith Undone*, p. 58.

39 Dan Kimbal, *The Emerging Church* (Grand Rapids, MI: Zondervan, 2003), 186.

40 McLaren, *A Generous Orthodoxy*, p. 175.

did the Apostle Paul say regarding the time period that would follow the apostolic generation? Was it a prediction of spiritual health and growth? No. Rather, he stated:

> I know that after my departure savage wolves will come in among you, not sparing the flock. (Acts 20:29)

We must not look for truth based on the practices found in church history, since Paul said specifically that false teachers would enter the church following the deaths of the apostles. If you want to seek truth, you go back to the apostolic generation itself.

The Dark Ages are becoming relevant again, because we are going back to them in many corners today.

The question, then, is: Why not go back to the very beginning? Where in Scripture are we told that it is essential to embrace ancient liturgical and contemplative practices?

In fact, look at these words of Christ—condemning these contemplative practices:

> And when you are praying, do not use meaningless repetition as the Gentiles do, for they suppose that they will be heard for their many words. (Matt. 6:7)

A Church in Need of Rescue

The Protestant Reformation got the church back on the road to Antioch. It turned us away from centuries of mysticism, steeped in the allegorization of Alexandria. How did the Protestant Reformers accomplish this monumental feat? What specific methodology did they employ? How far did it go? Was it far enough? We will begin to examine that in the next chapter.

CHAPTER 4

The Contribution of the Protestant Reformers

God sovereignly prepared the Reformers for the roles that they were to fulfill.

Most people date the beginning of the Reformation with Martin Luther on Oct. 31, 1517. While he probably had the biggest influence, there were also others that God raised up before him to lay the groundwork for later events.

John Wycliffe (1320—1384)

This is a name that you have probably heard, as his influence continues down to our time. He was involved in some of the earliest attempts to translate the Bible into English.

Wycliffe's goal was to put Scripture into the language of the common man, which contradicted all that the Roman Catholic Church stood for throughout the Middle Ages.

Because of his early influence, Wycliffe has been called *The Morning Star of the Reformation.*

John Huss (1369—1415)

Huss was basically attempting to do what Luther did, but was martyred as a result, and was not allowed to lead the influential life that Luther had. But he was a great preacher and pastor, and another early light of the Reformation.

The Advent of the Printing Press

The printing press began to be widely used in Europe during the 15th century—less than 100 years before Luther.

Once this innovation became widespread, people could take the ideas of the Reformers—and the words of Scripture itself—and print them for a mass audience.

Clearly, God put the innovation in place to allow the Reformers to overcome the negativity of the Dark Ages.

The invention of the printing press was, in many ways, comparable to the onset of the Internet in recent years. Now, there are a lot of bad things on the Internet, but there is also much that is great. For instance, the little church that I pastor can take messages and send them out to the entire world. Just a few decades ago, only big churches with huge budgets could do this type of thing. Now it is open to virtually everyone. The Internet has leveled the playing field.

In a similar way, thanks to the innovation of the printing press, God was setting the stage for the rapid transmission of the ideas behind the Protestant Reformation.

The Principle of Preparation

God always prepares His instruments. Before God uses anyone for anything, there is always a time of preparation.

We see this in the life of Moses. He lived to 120 years of age—from

1526 to 1406 B.C. For the first 40 years of his life, he was being trained in the palace of Pharaoh. He received the best education—natural training—that could be given (cf. Acts 7:20-22). He would later use this training to write the Pentateuch, or Torah—the first five books of the Hebrew Bible.

Many of us are familiar with the last 40 years of Moses' life—when he was used of God to lead the children of Israel on the Exodus out of Egypt and through the wilderness. God utilized him to give Israel the Law during this time, also (cf. Acts 7:30-38).

But what about those middle 40 years? They are covered in Stephen's synopsis of Moses' life in Acts 7:23-29. What was God doing with this man's life during this time period? Oddly enough, it began with Moses killing a man.

Moses had a human education, but he had not had a spiritual education yet. Moses realized his calling, so when he saw an Egyptian abusing a Hebrew, he took action. He took matters into his own hands and committed murder.

Moses at this point was very fleshly, and thought that he could do the work of God through human power. God therefore ushered him into a phase of his life where he spent 40 years shepherding sheep—in preparation for shepherding God's people later. He had all the education that was available in Egypt, but he needed a spiritual education in Midian, where he would learn humility and dependence upon God. And he received it right there where many of the events of the final 40 years would take place.

In fact, he needed as much time in each of those first two phases of his life as he would have left to shepherd God's people during the third and final segment. Those middle 40 years of his life would empty him of himself. Notice the contrast between the man at age 40 and at age 80 in Exodus 2:12 and 3:11, respectively. In Exodus 2:12, Moses was so self-confident that he even committed murder in God's name. However, in Exodus 3:11, he saw himself as unworthy to be Israel's deliverer. Such a change in attitude and character is directly attributable to the intervening 40 years in between these verses that he spent in Midian where he was emptied of himself.

In other words, Moses did not become Moses the lawgiver and leader until God prepared His instrument.

And that is how we must look at the Protestant Reformers, as well. How did God prepare them for their tasks?

The Preparation of Luther

Luther was consecrated to his religious beliefs from an early age. Caught in a lightning storm and fearing death, Luther cried out to God (possibly to St. Anne) and promised to serve God his entire life if He would protect him.

Luther, like Calvin later, already had a background in studying law.[41] Law school trains lawyers in the literal, historical, grammatical method of interpretation. That is what Antioch taught regarding Scripture for the church's first two centuries. And that is the method that Luther and Calvin would use to rescue the church from allegorical interpretation—in certain areas. That legal training is part of who the Protestant Reformers were via Divine preparation.

Following the storm incident, Luther took a vow of poverty to enter the monastery. But here he began to question why the Roman Catholic Church was living at such a high material level when he and his fellow monks were living at such a low level—supposedly out of necessity in their monastic service to God.

Luther joined an Augustinian monastery—the strictest order available. He could only speak once a day. He had to wear an irritating, bristling sweater. And he would come to confess his sins four times per day—sometimes for two hours or more at a time, thereby all but exhausting the priests, to whom

41 Alan W. Gomes, *Reformation & Modern Theology and Historical Theology Survey Course Syllabus* (La Mirada: Biola Bookstore, 1999), p. 23; Justo L. Gonzáles, *The Story of Christianity: The Reformation to the Present Day* (San Francisco, CA: Harper Collins, 1985), p. 62; Dave Hunt, *What Love Is This? Calvinism's Misrepresentation of God*, 4th ed. (Bend, OR: Berean Call, 2013), p. 40.

he regularly confessed his sins.

But he discovered that, no matter how harshly he treated his body, it was to no avail in finding relief for his tortured soul. And he was still a very angry man.

Luther was discovering what the Apostle Paul told the Colossian church:

> If you have died with Christ to the elementary principles of the world, why, as if you were living in the world, do you submit yourself to decrees, such as, "Do not handle, do not taste, do not touch!" (which all *refer to* things destined to perish with use)—in accordance with the commandments and teachings of men? These are matters which have, to be sure, the appearance of wisdom in self-made religion and self-abasement and severe treatment of the body, *but are* of no value against fleshly indulgence. (Col. 2:20-23)

No matter what type of monastic deprivation you put your body under, your sin nature is still there. You do not really know that until you put yourself under monasticism and see its total inability to control the sin nature. What you need in order to control the sin nature is to be baptized spiritually into Christ and receive the new resources which are provided by the Holy Spirit.

The hand of God was at work preparing Martin Luther. And this soon led to Luther's conversion.

His superiors sought to more productively redirect young Luther's seemingly boundless energy by putting him to work translating from the Greek New Testament and teaching the newest monastery students. And that led to his discovery of the book of Galatians!

He began reading things like this:

> Nevertheless knowing that a man is not justified by the works of the Law but through faith in Christ Jesus, even we have believed in Christ Jesus, so that we may be justified by faith in Christ and

> not by the works of the Law; since by the works of the Law no flesh will be justified. (Gal. 2:16)

This was counterintuitive to everything that Luther had experienced. But there was more:

> I have been crucified with Christ; and it is no longer I who live, but Christ lives in me; and the *life* which I now live in the flesh I live by faith in the Son of God, who loved me and gave Himself up for me. (Gal. 2:20)

> Are you so foolish? Having begun by the Spirit, are you now being perfected by the flesh? (Gal. 3:3)

> But I say, walk by the Spirit, and you will not carry out the desire of the flesh. (Gal. 5:16)

Luther was coming to understand that monasticism, depravation and other harsh treatments of the body will not help anyone control the sin nature. Only the Holy Spirit can do that.

This time of study, translation and teaching was revolutionary in Luther's life. He began to call the book of Galatians *meine frau*—my wife! He was wedded to the book of Galatians because of the revolution that he was experiencing. That is why he would become so pro-Scripture in his subsequent debates with the Catholic church. He was seeing in the Scriptures things that are the opposite of all that he experienced in monasticism.

The Reformation began with Luther nailing his 95 theses to the Castle Church door in Wittenberg, Germany, on Oct. 31, 1517.

At that point, Luther was not attempting to begin a Protestant movement. He was attempting, as a professor, to begin a conversation. He intended to remain Roman Catholic. He never wanted to break away and begin something new—although he was ultimately forced into that by the actions of the Roman Catholic Church. They questioned him as a heretic. Yet, he found a groundswell of support from the poor and the working class, who had been suppressed and abused by the existing Roman Catholic system through the sale of indulgences, among other things.

The Stress on Literal Interpretation

William Tyndale, a contemporary of Martin Luther who lived from 1494 to 1536, stated:

> The Scripture hath but one sense, which is the literal sense.[42]

That is the exact opposite of what the Roman Catholic Church had been teaching, based on the foundation that went back to Alexandria, Egypt, for more than 1,000 years.

There is one interpretation of Scripture, although there can be many applications. We find this theme running throughout Luther's sermons and writings. He said:

> [The Scriptures] are to be retained in their simplest meaning ever possible, and to be understood in their grammatical and literal sense unless the context plainly forbids.[43]

This is the literal method of interpretation—taking words and ideas in the Bible in their ordinary sense unless there is something in the context that tells us that the Scriptural writers are using figures of speech.

The Bible does use figures of speech, such as hyperbole, similes, metaphors and personification (cf. Ps. 98:8; Isa. 55:12). But these are obvious in the text itself. Otherwise, we must take the Bible for what it says. This is the method that Luther used to restore the church to proper doctrine, which

---

42 William Tyndale, "Obedience of a Christian Man," in *Doctrinal Treatises and Introductions to Different Portions of the Holy Scriptures*, ed. Henry Walter (Cambridge: Cambridge University Press, 1848), p. 304.

43 Martin Luther, *Luther's Works*, 6:509; Quoted by Roy B. Zuck, *Basic Bible Interpretation: A Practical Guide to Discovering Biblical Truth* (Colorado Springs, CO: Victor, 1991), p. 45.

had been lost to the church for more than 1,000 years.

He stated:

> I have observed this, that all heresies and errors have originated, not from the simple words of Scripture, as is so universally asserted, but from *neglecting* the simple words of Scripture, and from the affection of purely subjective . . . tropes and inferences.
>
> In the schools of theologians it is a well-known rule that Scripture is to be understood in four ways, literal, allegoric, moral, anagogic. But if we wish to handle Scripture aright, our one effort will be to obtain *unum, simplecum, germanum, et certum sensum literalem.*
>
> Each passage has one clear, definite, and true sense of its own. All others are but doubtful and uncertain opinions.[44]

Luther is getting back to the objective truth of God's Word, which everyone can understand. All of the concepts that allegorical interpretation foists upon the Scripture are simply subjective opinion.

But Luther, by such statements, is disrupting more than 1,000 years of church authority.

Peters records:

> Thus Luther (*Table Talk*, "On God's Word," 11) remarks: "I have grounded my preaching upon the literal word; he that pleases may follow me, he that will not may stay."[45]

Notice how Luther keeps using this word *literal.* According to the *Oxford English Dictionary*, the meaning of *literal* is basically *by the letters*. That means that you are interpreting what is there, rather than dragging external ideas into the passage.

---

44 Martin Luther, quoted in Frederic W. Farrar, *History of Interpretation* (Grand Rapids: Baker, 1961; reprint, 1886), p. 327.

45 Martin Luther, *Table Talk*, "On God's Word," 11; Quoted by George N. H. Peters, *The Theocratic Kingdom*, 3 vols. (New York: Funk & Wagnalls, 1884; reprint, Grand Rapids: Kregel, 1952), 1:47.

Calvin and Literal Interpretation

Calvin says much the same things as Luther about literal interpretation. Zuck notes:

> Calvin wrote in the preface of his commentary on Romans "it is the first business of an interpreter to let the author say what he does say, instead of attributing to him what we think he ought to say."[46]

We may take this for granted, but after 1,000 years of allegorization—when people had no Bibles to read at all—these were revolutionary statements. And God was using it to redirect the church away from Roman Catholicism, Augustinianism and Alexandrianism and lead the way back to Antioch.

Zuck records again:

> Calvin wrote in his commentary on Galatians "Let us know then that the true meaning of Scripture is the natural and obvious meaning; and let us embrace and abide by it resolutely."[47]

Calvin is telling us to take the words and phrases of the Bible literally in their context. Their meanings are the ones they would normally have in ordinary speaking, writing and thinking. Do not assign meanings to words which they do not normally carry. If you are not willing to do that, then the authority in interpretation changes. It moves away from the Biblical text to the subjective mind of the interpreter. Thus, the whole issue of consistent literal interpretation is simply a battle of authority. Will the written Word of God rule out, or will it be the mind of the allegorist?

Church historian Philip Schaff writes:

---

46 John Calvin; Quoted by Zuck, *Basic Bible Interpretation*, 47.

47 John Calvin, *Commentary on the Epistle of Paul to the Galatians*, p. 136; Quoted in Gerrit H. Hospers, *The Principle of Spiritualization in Hermeneutics* (East Williamson, NY: Author, 1935), p. 11.

> Calvin is the founder of grammatico–historical exegesis. He affirmed and carried out the sound hermeneutical principle the biblical writers, like all sensible writers, wished to convey to their readers—one definite thought in words which they could understand. A passage may have a literal or figurative sense; but cannot have two senses at once. The Word of God is inexhaustible and applicable to all times, but there is a difference between explanation and application, and application must be consistent with explanation.[48]

I believe that Calvin is more aptly described as the retriever of literal, historical, grammatical exegesis. Nevertheless, Schaff's quote points out how Calvin and the Reformers took the church back to studying the laws of language—utilizing the proper understanding of syntax and *grammatical* sentence structure. Remember, God has revealed Himself in language. He is the author of language, and created the laws that govern it.

The Bible was written in a specific *historical* context. We must interpret the words based on how they were commonly used at the time of their writing.

Going by the very letters of Scripture (*literal*), Luther and Calvin practiced *exegesis*. For the previous 1,000 years, the church had practiced *eisegesis*. Again, it was a question of authority.

The Reformers restored this method in some areas of the Bible. As we will see later, sadly, they did not do it in other areas. But at least they gave us a start!

The Reformers, in essence, knocked over a domino. And once it fell, the Holy Spirit raised up others who could go even further and knock over more dominoes—using the same method that the Protestant Reformers retrieved from Antioch.

Note well the principle that the Reformers gave back to us: Interpretation is one, applications are many. The first goal of the interpreter

48 Philip Schaff; Quoted by Hospers, *The Principle of Spiritualization in Hermeneutics*, p. 12.

is to understand the meaning of the text. Once you figure that out, then the next thing to do is to apply that meaning to the needs of the audience. You may apply the same text in many different ways—but never outside of its established meaning.

You cannot utilize this method of interpretation, through expository preaching, in sound bites. It takes time to stand in the pulpit and establish the meaning of the text. People today just want application. The problem with this is that people leave with wonderful application, but they do not know where it came from. It will make them feel better for a short time, but when the first trial comes up, it will simply dissolve like cotton candy.

Application is an important step in the process—but it is a secondary step. People need to understand, first and foremost, the meaning of the text. The application is only as good as the meaning from which it comes.

Condemnation of Allegorization

The Reformers emphasized literal interpretation and condemned allegorization.

Farrar stated:

> Luther denounced the allegorical approach to Scripture in strong words. He said: "An interpreter . . . must as much as possible avoid allegory, that he may not wander in idle dreams." "Allegories are empty speculations and as it were the scum of Holy Scripture." "Origen's allegories are not worth so much dirt." "To allegorize is to juggle with Scripture." "Allegory is sort of a beautiful harlot, who proves herself specially seductive to idle men." "Allegorizing may degenerate into a mere monkey game." "Allegories are awkward, absurd, inventive, obsolete, loose rags . . . mere spangles and pretty ornaments but nothing more."[49]

49 Martin Luther; Quoted in Farrar, *History of Interpretation*, p. 328.

You can see from this quotation why the Roman Catholic hierarchy reacted to Luther in the way that it did.

We find the same type of aggressive denunciation of allegorization in the writings of Calvin. According to Zuck:

> Calvin similarly rejected allegorical interpretations. He called them "frivolous games" and accused Origen and other allegorists of "torturing scripture, in every possible sense, from the true sense."[50]

In other words, allegorists are ignoring the laws which govern all language. Since God has revealed Himself in language, you must understand those laws in order to understand Him. Ignoring those laws would be as foolish as ignoring the laws of gravity.

Rejection of Church Tradition as a Guide

Because of their focus on literal interpretation, the Reformers began to reject the authority of church tradition as a guide. They followed the words of Jesus, who faced this same battle with the Pharisees.

The Pharisees had buried the Scriptures under many layers of manmade tradition. To read the detailed writings that they follow, the Mishnah and the Talmud, is simply exhausting. It was originally well-intentioned, but after a time their regulations began to overtake the interpretive process. The text itself was no longer being interpreted, but was being filtered through layers of Pharisaical regulations. Thus, the text was no longer their ultimate authority—and the regulations ultimately led to the loss of the meaning of the text.

Jesus chided the Pharisees, saying:

> *Thus* invalidating the word of God by your tradition which you have handed down; and you do many things such as that. (Mark 7:13)

50 John Calvin; Quoted by Zuck, *Basic Bible Interpretation*, p. 47.

He emphasized the authority of the Scriptures, and that is basically what the Reformers had to do also. Jesus stood against the traditions of the Pharisees; Luther and Calvin stood against the Roman Catholic hierarchy and its traditions.

Luther made many statements against using church tradition as a guide. His most famous is this one, which he made at the Diet of Worms:

> Unless I am convinced by Scripture and plain reason—I do not accept the authority of the popes and councils, for they have contradicted each other—my conscience is captive to the Word of God. I cannot and I will not recant anything for to go against conscience is neither right nor safe. God help me. Amen.[51]

The interesting thing about manmade traditions is that they frequently depart from God's Word. Thus, when they departed from God's written Word, Luther (like Jesus) departed from them.

We face this same situation today. People still desire to follow traditions. The issue is: Is this tradition in harmony with the Scripture? You will not be able to answer that question unless you have read and understood the Scripture.

Here is one of my favorite quotes from Luther, in his debate with Dr. Johann Eck:

> I ask for the Scripture, and Eck offers me the Fathers. I ask for the sun, and he shows me his lanterns. I ask, "where is your Scripture proof?" and he adduces Ambrose and Cyril. . . . With all due respect to the Fathers, I prefer the authority of Scripture.[52]

Eck was looking for his authority to church councils, creeds, confessions, monks, priests and popes. But Luther looked to one church father that

51 Martin Luther, Luther at the Imperial Diet of Worms (1521).

52 Martin Luther; Quoted in Farrar, *History of Interpretation*, p. 327.

outweighs every other church father, which is the Apostle Paul! He continues to quote Romans and Galatians, and rejects church tradition as a guide.

That includes the rejection of the papacy. In the Roman Catholic system, the pope has the ability to speak *ex cathedra*—"from the chair." Such proclamations are placed on equal authority with the Word of God. They trace the lineage of the papacy to Peter, who they believe to be the first pope.

When you talk to a Roman Catholic friend, you must understand that you are operating by a different authority base than they are. That is why we disagree on so many things. They have additional authority outside of Scripture.

In Matthew 16:18, Jesus is speaking to Peter, saying:

> I also say to you that you are Peter, and upon this rock I will build My church; and the gates of Hades will not overpower it.

Roman Catholics teach that Jesus built the church on Peter, the first pope. That is a problem though, because we read five verses later that Peter's mouth was about to be used as an instrument of Satan. Christ stated:

> But He turned and said to Peter, "Get behind Me, Satan! You are a stumbling block to Me; for you are not setting your mind on God's interests, but man's." (Matt. 16:23)

As we have already noted, in the original Greek, it is very clear that Jesus is building the church—not upon Peter himself, but upon his accurate confession of the truth about Christ:

> He said to them, "But who do you say that I am?" Simon Peter answered, "You are the Christ, the Son of the living God." And Jesus said to him, "Blessed are you, Simon Barjona, because flesh and blood did not reveal *this* to you, but My Father who is in heaven." (Matt. 16:15-17)

The Protestant Reformers boldly rejected church tradition as a guide and went back to interpreting the Bible through the lens of literal interpretation, rather than through the lens of the papacy.

The Five Solas

Sola is a Latin word meaning "by itself." Out of the Protestant Reformation comes an emphasis on five major truths:

Sola Scriptura—Scripture Alone
Solus Christus—Christ Alone
Sola Fide—Faith Alone
Sola Gratia—Grace Alone
Soli Deo Gloria—To the Glory of God Alone

Using the literal method of interpretation, the Reformers found these important concepts in the Bible. Let us examine each of them.

Sola Scriptura

Scripture, by itself, is our authority. This is why Luther can speak as he did at Worms, as we have seen:

> Unless I am convinced by Scripture and plain reason—I do not accept the authority of the popes and councils, for they have contradicted each other—my conscience is captive to the Word of God.[53]

His entire thinking was based on Scripture by itself.

This truth is being erased today by the emergent church, which is going back to the pre-Reformation Dark Ages. Consider this quote from emergent church advocate Brian McLaren:

> Anglicans have demonstrated this "both-and" beautifully in relation to Scripture. Scripture is always a factor in Anglican

53 Martin Luther, Luther at the Imperial Diet of Worms (1521).

> thinking. In Anglicans' best moments, it is their primary factor, but it is never . . . the only factor. Rather Scripture is always in dialogue with tradition, reason, and experience. None of them "sola" can be the ultimate source of authority. . . .[54]

McLaren is telling us that *tradition*, *reason* and *experience* each hold an invaluable place in establishing our *authority*. But is this really true?

The Bible addresses the weakness and potential pitfalls involved with each of these categories:

Tradition—Mark 7:13; Col. 2:8

Reason—Prov. 3:5; 14:12; Isa. 55:8-9

Experience—2 Thess. 2:9

None of these things can be placed on the same level as the Bible in terms of our authority. Notice what the Apostle Paul says:

> So then, brethren, stand firm and hold to the traditions which you were taught, whether by word *of mouth* or by letter from us. (2 Thess. 2:15)

Tradition is not always bad; it can be a very helpful thing if it is consistent with the Bible. But the Bible condemns making it more important than Scripture itself. When tradition departs from Scripture, we must depart from tradition.

Furthermore, if total depravity is true, then even my mental capacity is tainted by sin, and I cannot fully trust my reason, either.

As brilliant as the human mind may become with the capacities that God has given it, our reasoning can also go astray. This is why we are told repeatedly to test our intellectual conclusions by the Word of God. God may also do things that are beyond my mental capacities to understand. Thus, human reason itself must always be held to a subservient role relative to the plain declarations of Scripture. Theologian Louis Berkhof well articulates

54 Brian McLaren, *A Generous Orthodoxy* (Grand Rapids: Zondervan, 2004), p. 210.

this principle when he says:

> Since the entrance of sin into the world, man can gather true knowledge about God from his general revelation only if he studies it in light of Scripture, in which the elements of God's original self-revelation, which were obscured and perverted by the blight of sin, are published, corrected, and interpreted. ... Some are inclined to speak of God's revelation as a second source; but this is hardly correct in view of the fact that nature can come into consideration here only as interpreted in the light of Scripture.[55]

Our experience cannot be our guide either; it is not equal with the Bible. In fact, we see throughout Scripture how Satan and his demons are given the authority to perform certain miracles (cf. Ex. 7-8; Deut. 13:1-3; Matt. 7:21-23; 24:24; Acts 8:9; 16:16; Gal. 1:6-9).

Some people think that whatever experience they have had must be from God. But this is not true—the devil can give us experiences, too. In fact, the greatest signs and wonders movement predicted in the pages of God's Word is the false signs and wonders movement of the antichrist (cf. Rev. 13:3, 13; 16:13-14).

Experience cannot be a test of truth unless the experience aligns with Scripture. We must hold all other things loosely against the authority of Scripture, and use them in a *ministerial* sense, not a *magisterial* sense. They do not sit in judgment on the Bible, but are rather in a subservient role, serving to explain and illustrate Biblical realities.

For the Reformers, the authority base is the Bible, and the Bible alone.

---

55 Louis Berkhof, introductory volume to *Systematic Theology* (Grand Rapids: Eerdman's, 1946), pp. 60, 96.

Solus Christus

Salvation is found in *Christ alone*. Adding that word *sola* here is what put the Reformers at war with the Catholic hierarchy. If they had just left that word out, everyone would have been happy. But their emphasis went against 1,000 years of tradition in the Dark Ages.

John 14:6 states:

> Jesus said to him, "I am the way, and the truth, and the life; no one comes to the Father but through Me."

Acts 4:12 reveals:

> And there is salvation in no one else; for there is no other name under heaven that has been given among men by which we must be saved.

1 Timothy 2:5 records:

> For there is one God, *and* one mediator also between God and men, *the* man Christ Jesus.

Christ is the only one who can mediate between God and man, because His is the only one who is both God and man!

The Reformers thus rejected Mariolatry. Mary was the virgin mother of Jesus, having been used by the Holy Spirit in Jesus' conception in order to bring Him into the world. We respect her and honor her, but we do not pray to her. She was not God, so any prayer offered to her has no power and is of no validity. It is empty tradition. We must never elevate her to a place which the Bible does not give to her.

The Reformers rejected the Roman Catholic notion of the sinless perfection of Mary. Mary was not sinless (cf. Rom. 3:23). Instead, her own testimony is seen in this passage where Mary herself indicated her need of a Savior:

> And Mary said:
> "My soul exalts the Lord,
> And my spirit has rejoiced in God *my Savior.*" (Luke 1:46-47; italics added)

The Reformers also rejected the idea of the perpetual virginity of Mary. The Bible tells us that, indeed, she and Joseph had other children in addition to Jesus (cf. Matt. 13:55). Two of them, James and Jude, wrote books of the New Testament. We refer to them as the half-brothers of Christ since they shared the same mother as the Savior, but not the same biological father.

Being born of a virgin, Jesus did not inherit a human sin nature, but instead uniquely qualified to be our sinless sacrifice, which God would accept (cf. Exod. 12:5; John 1:29).

On the basis of *sola Scriptura*, the Reformers realized and taught the truth of *solus Christus*.

Sola Fide

Sola fide is the idea that you are saved through the power of Christ on the basis of one condition—which is faith alone in Christ alone. The Bible teaches this more than 160 times.

Abraham was justified by faith (cf. Gen. 15:6). It is not contrition, repentance for personal sin, walking an aisle or giving money to a cause that justifies one before God. There is only one command for the lost sinner to fulfill in order to be right with God (cf. John 3:16; Acts 16:30-31), and this is to believe in the one (Jesus Christ) that "He has sent" (John 6:28-29).

Consider these important Scriptures:

> For by grace you have been saved through faith; and that not of yourselves, *it is* the gift of God; not as a result of works, so that no one may boast. (Eph. 2:8-9)

> And without faith it is impossible to please *Him*, for he

> who comes to God must believe that He is and *that* He is a rewarder of those who seek Him. (Heb. 11:6)

Sola Gratia

This next *sola* means that we are saved by grace alone. Grace is unmerited favor—coming from God to a lost sinner, who did not work for it and does not deserve it.

Righteousness is transferred to the account of the believing sinner at the point of faith. Luther called this "the great exchange," in which the sinner's unrighteousness is exchanged for Christ's righteousness in a single instant, and God looks at you as if you were just as righteous as Jesus.

Do you realize this? If you are in Christ, then when God the Father looks at you, He sees your position as being just as righteous as Jesus (cf. 2 Cor. 5:21; Phil. 3:9)!

But you say, "I do not deserve this! I fail all the time." Ah, but that is why it is called *grace*—the best deal in the universe.

Do you see how these *solas* are linked? Notice Romans 4:4-5:

> Now to the one who works, his wage is not credited as a favor, but as what is due. *But to the one who does not work, but believes in Him who justifies the ungodly*, his faith is credited as righteousness. (italics added)

Believing—exercising faith—is the only thing that a lost sinner can do before a holy God in order to gain His favor. But faith is not a work. And since we receive all of these great blessings by faith alone, therefore they come to us by grace (unmerited favor) alone.

Soli Deo Gloria

The fifth and final sola is soli deo gloria—to the glory of God alone.

Johann Sebastian Bach famously included the letters SDG on his musical works—showing that he was writing them solely for God's glory.

If salvation is a grace operation from beginning to end, and the only thing that you did to gain access to it is something that is non meritorious (exercising faith), then who gets the glory for all of it? God does!

This shows the danger of subtly mixing works with the gospel. Yet this is in man's nature, so we must strive to always keep the gospel pure.

Many Christians develop a method of sharing the gospel that may have several steps to it. But the moment that you add a single step other than faith you are adding things to the Word of God that are simply not there.

God convicts the sinner by His Holy Spirit, and educates the person in His truth to make that person aware that he or she is a sinner. At that point, the only thing that God asks a lost sinner to do is to believe. This is all that is required in order to be justified. We must be careful never to add things that God has not required. The Protestant Reformers understood this very clearly.

You see, if salvation is based on grace alone, through faith alone, in Christ alone—then my hand cannot be raised to share part of the glory. All of the glory goes to God alone. If anything at all were to be added to that faith, then a human being could share in that glory. But that is not possible. God has set it up in a way that there are no human bragging rights.

Isaiah 42:8 states:

> I am the Lord, that is My name;
> I will not give My glory to another,
> Nor My praise to graven images.

There is always a struggle to keep the gospel clear, because prideful man wants to add to it so that he can get part of the credit.

But Ephesians 2:9 concludes with the words: "so that no one may boast." If salvation is a grace operation from beginning to end, it gives human beings no boasting rights at all. This is why Galatians 5:11 speaks of "the stumbling block of the cross." My pride makes me want to contribute to my own salvation. But God has set the whole thing up so that boasting, which would spring from any such effort, is eliminated.

As the Apostle Paul stated again:

> Where then is boasting? It is excluded. By what kind of law? Of works? No, but by a law of faith. For we maintain that a man is justified by faith apart from works of the Law. (Rom. 3:27-28)

The Priesthood of All Believers

In addition to the five solas, there is another great area that the Reformers began to restore to the church.

In the Roman Catholic system, you confess your sins to a priest—your intermediary between you and God. This was another reason, people were told, that they could not understand the Bible. That was the role of the priest.

But the priests were greatly abusing this role through such things as the sale of indulgences.

The Roman priests actually had no Scriptural authority at all for what they were doing, because of passages like this which were written to the church:

> He has made us *to be* a kingdom, priests to His God and Father—to Him *be* the glory and the dominion forever and ever. Amen. (Rev. 1:6)

Every true believer is a priest during this age of the church.

In Old Testament Israel, not everyone was a priest—or could become a priest. The priests came from the tribe of Levi, and had to be descendants of the lineage of Aaron.

But during the church age, beginning in Acts 2, there is a different teaching for this dispensation.

Believer, did you know that you are a priest? This is a startling discovery to make! Each believer has the ability to understand the Bible on his or her own.

Sometimes, however, believers today may still carry some remnants of Roman Catholic thought—such as assigning to a pastor something akin to the status of a priest.

Although there are different roles, as God gives to some the gifts to be pastor-teachers, every single believer is a priest and possesses the same authoritative standing before God.

Every Christian has access to God and can understand the Bible. As Peter states:

> But you are A CHOSEN RACE, A royal PRIESTHOOD, A HOLY NATION, A PEOPLE FOR *God's* OWN POSSESSION, so that you may proclaim the excellencies of Him who has called you out of darkness into His marvelous light; for you once were NOT A PEOPLE, but now you are THE PEOPLE OF GOD; you had NOT RECEIVED MERCY, but now you have RECEIVED MERCY. (1 Pet. 2:9-10)

Soon other dominoes would begin to fall, as well.

New Translations of the Bible

If all believers are priests, and the Bible is literally true, and God gave us a book to understand, then it follows naturally that it is necessary to translate the Bible into the language of the common man.

This is difficult for us to envision, because the Bible is so totally accessible to us today. But in the day of the Reformers, it had not been accessible for 1,000 years.

Luther translated the New Testament in 11 months—not from *Latin* into German, but from *Greek* into German. The Latin Vulgate had been available since the days of the fourth century and Jerome. But Luther did not trust the Roman Catholic version. He wanted to give the people a Bible in their own language, but translated from the original language.

Luther later spent 11 years translating the Old Testament from Hebrew into German.

Tyndale was doing this same thing in English, and his work has become the basis for all English translations since that time, for which we should be most grateful.

An Emphasis on Literacy

But all of this translation does no one any good if people cannot read. The Reformers faced a population affected by rampant illiteracy, and consequently had to raise the literacy standard.

The Reformers began to emphasize literacy so that people could read the Bible for themselves. This was based on the theological rubric of the priesthood of all believers.

This required the establishment of schools. And that leads to another great quote from Martin Luther—which was nearly prophetic!

> I am afraid that the schools will prove the very gates of hell, unless they diligently labor in explaining the Holy Scriptures and engraving them in the heart of the youth. . . . I advise no one to place his child where the Scriptures do not reign paramount. Every institution in which men are not unceasingly occupied with the Word of God must become corrupt.[56]

This emphasis is lived out in our day in the Christian school and homeschool movements. If they could be resurrected from the dead today, the Reformers would be the most enthusiastic cheerleaders of these movements.

The subsequent generations of those impacted by the Reformation came from Europe to America. This country was, in fact, founded by the

56 Martin Luther, *Luther's Works: The Christian in Society*, ed. James Atkinson, vol. 44 (Philadelphia, PA: Fortress, 1966), p. 207.

children, the spiritual descendants, of the Protestant Reformation.

They came here with the same mindset, and this led to the establishment of the American public school system.

We see the heritage of the Reformers in laws such as this one, which formed the beginning of public schools in this country:

> It being one chief project of that old deluder, Satan, to keep men from the knowledge of the Scriptures, *as in former time*. . . . It is therefore ordered . . . that after the Lord hath increased the settlement . . . they shall . . . appoint one within their town, to teach all such children to read . . . they shall set up a grammar school to instruct youths. . . .[57] (italics added)

The *former time* here is the Dark Ages when the Scripture was inaccessible to the common man largely due to illiteracy. They did not want to go back to them. That required having literate people, which required reading teachers who could teach the laws of language to the *youths*. This is the origin of public education in the United States. We have so lost sight of this history so that we cannot even see through the lies today of those who seek to secularize our public schools in front of our very faces. In sum, the Reformers' doctrine of the *priesthood of all believers* led to the need for translations of the Bible in the language of the common man, but it also had the effect of raising literacy standards for the entire population. Thus, what we have today in terms of Bible translations, as well as public education, is largely due to the positive influence of the Protestant Reformers.

Impact on America

What a heritage we have in the Reformation! If the Protestant Reformation had not happened, I do not believe that that the system of government that

57 Old Satan Deluder Law: 1642 Massachusetts, *Church of the Holy Trinity v. U.S.*, 143 U.S. 457, 467 (1892).

we have in the United States would exist. The default mode of governments throughout human history is totalitarianism, and that is probably what we would have in this country were it not for our heritage in the Reformation.

Our system of government is totally unique, and our founding documents have allowed us to enjoy political freedom over a long period of time. But these documents make no sense unless you view them through the lens of the Protestant Reformation.

The most important book that has ever been written is the Bible. The second most important document that has ever been created, in my opinion, is the United States Constitution—including the Bill of Rights. Our Constitution certainly is not Divinely inspired in the Biblical sense, but it has given people more political and economic freedom than any other document in the history of the human race.

Our system of government divides power and creates checks and balances for each branch of government, so no one branch can get control of everything. Former Supreme Court Justice Antonin Scalia (1936–2016) well explains the uniqueness of America's Constitution:

> Every tin horn dictator in the world today, every president for life, has a Bill of Rights...That's not what makes us free; if it did, you would rather live in Zimbabwe. But you wouldn't want to live in most countries in the world that have a Bill of Rights. What has made us free is our Constitution. Think of the word "constitution;" it means "structure." That's why America's framers debated, not the Bill of Rights during the Constitutional Convention of 1787 in Philadelphia ... but rather the structure of the federal government. The genius of the American constitutional system is the dispersal of power. Once power is centralized in one person, or one part [of government], a Bill of Rights is just words on paper. A constitution is about setting structure; it is not about writing the preferences of special interest groups.[58]

58 Kevin Mooney, "Supreme Court Justice Scalia: Constitution, Not Bill of Rights, Makes Us Free," May 11 2015, http://dailysignal.com/2015/05/11/supreme-court-justice-scalia-constitution-not-

Our Founding Fathers not only divided power in this way, horizontally, but they also divided it vertically—by creating multiple state governments, as opposed to only a single national government. In fact, if you study the material from our founding, you will find that the true source of power is really to rest in these state governments.

There is not a business man upon planet Earth who would set his business up in this way. It is deliberately designed to be inefficient. That is why it is always humorous to hear people complain that there is too much gridlock in government, or that nothing is getting done. It was purposely designed to create gridlock! That is the point. We ought to be grateful, for the most part, that nothing is getting done—because that is a guarantee that our freedoms remain intact. I do not want to live in a country where things get done at the snap of someone's fingers. That is the mark of totalitarianism—where things get done without any input from the people.

If our government had been set up by people who believed that human beings were naturally and inherently good at heart, they would never have set up this type of inefficient system. The reason that we have this deliberately cumbersome system is because of a belief that came from the Protestant Reformation called *total depravity*.

This, of course, is the first point of *TULIP*—the five points of the Calvinistic system.[59]

One does not necessarily have to endorse all points of this system in order to understand and appreciate these truths and how they impacted the establishment of our government in the United States.

The descendants of the Reformation did not believe in the perfectibility of human nature. Rather, by total depravity, they meant that sin has corrupted every part of my being—even my intellect and capacity for thought.

Luther believed strongly in *The Bondage of the Will*—the title of his

bill-of-rights-makes-us-free/; Internet; accessed 20 January 2016.

59 The other points are: unconditional election, limited atonement, irresistible grace and perseverance of the saints.

most important book. I believe that some of what he wrote in that book was overstated. But what Luther believed is that sin has not merely corrupted humanity from the neck down, but rather the effect of sin is so pervasive that it has affected how we think.

The Apostle Paul stated in Romans 3:11 (quoting Ps. 14:2 and 53:2):

> THERE IS NONE WHO UNDERSTANDS,
> THERE IS NONE WHO SEEKS FOR GOD.

He also reminded us of the influence that the devil has been allowed to have:

> In whose case the god of this world has blinded the minds of the unbelieving so that they might not see the light of the gospel of the glory of Christ, who is the image of God. (2 Cor. 4:4)

We find this truth going all the way back to the book of Genesis:

> The LORD smelled the soothing aroma; and the LORD said to Himself, "I will never again curse the ground on account of man, for *the intent of man's heart is evil from his youth*; and I will never again destroy every living thing, as I have done." (Gen. 8:21; italics added)

From the point of conception, the sin nature is handed down to every single human being:

> Behold, I was brought forth in iniquity,
> And in sin my mother conceived me. (Ps. 51:5)

Both the rulers, as well as the masses, possess such a sin nature. If you believe that, it shapes your view of government. As Lord Acton stated:

> All power tends to corrupt and absolute power corrupts absolutely.[60]

60 Lord Acton, "Letter to Bishop Mandell Creighton," April 5, 1887, published in *Historical Essays and Studies*, edited by J. N. Figgis and R. V. Laurence (London: Macmillan, 1907). This letter can be accessed at https://history.hanover.edu/courses/excerpts/165acton.html.

In the Greek system, the people running the government were viewed as demigods. But the Bible teaches that everyone has been corrupted by this sin nature. So, the last thing that you would want to do is centralize power in the hands of one person.

We see this illustrated in the book of Genesis. Following the statement of Genesis 8:21, we find in Genesis 11 the tower of Babel, and the attempt to consolidate power under Nimrod, who was attempting to take over the world. God disrupted it by confusing the peoples' language, which created a check and balance system:

> So the LORD scattered them abroad from there over the face of the whole earth; and they stopped building the city. Therefore its name was called Babel, because there the LORD confused the language of the whole earth; and from there the LORD scattered them abroad over the face of the whole earth. (Gen. 11:8-9)

What you believe about human nature will control your philosophy of government. We can see this in the writings called *The Federalist Papers*, which were written to the common people—at the reading level of the average farmer (the intellectual capacities of people were much higher at the time of our founding). They were written for the purpose of convincing the people of New York to ratify the Constitution, and they shed light on the basis of our government.

James Madison, "the chief architect of the United States Constitution," wrote in *Federalist No. 51*:

> But what is government but the greatest of all reflections on human nature? If men were angels, no government would be necessary. If angels were to govern men, neither external nor internal controls on government would be necessary. In framing a government which is to be administered by men over men, the great difficulty lies in this: you must first enable the

> government to control the governed; and in the next place oblige it to control itself.[61]

In sum, without the Reformers' emphasis on the Scriptural doctrine of *total depravity*, America's governing construct of separation of powers, which has allowed us to avoid totalitarianism, would not exist. One of the few people I have seen who have developed this idea is Loraine Boettner, who quotes many historians to establish this point:

> Bancroft "... simply calls Calvin 'the father of America' and adds: 'He who will not honor the memory and respect the influence of Calvin knows but little of the origin of American liberty.'"[62]

Doubtless the Reformers themselves did not realize all that they were actually putting in motion through the movement that they began, which returned the focus to Holy Scripture. Among other things, they originated a philosophy of political science of which we are the beneficiaries. Of course, God was always in the background of history, sovereignly connecting together the various links in the chain.

If you enjoy your freedoms in America, you ought to thank the Lord for Martin Luther and John Calvin.

Rejection of Celibacy for Ministers

Prior to this point, and even in Roman Catholic tradition today, if you really desire to serve God you must remain single. You cannot be married.

Remember that the Roman Catholic Church called Peter the first pope, based on a misinterpretation of this verse:

---

61 Alexander Hamilton, James Madison and John Jay, *The Federalist Papers*, trans. Clinton Rossiter (New York: Penguin, 1961), p. 322.

62 Loraine Boettner, *The Reformed Doctrine of Predestination* (Philipsburg, NJ: Presbyterian and Reformed, 1932), pp. 398-390.

> I also say to you that you are Peter, and upon this rock I will build My church; and the gates of Hades will not overpower it. (Matt. 16:18)

But Peter was not the first pope, as we have previously seen. Christ did not build the church on Peter—the man who denied the Lord three times (cf. Matt. 26: 69-75). He became a great man of God, but he certainly had feet of clay.

We also know that Peter himself was, indeed, married. According to Mathew 8:14, Peter had a mother-in-law, something that would be impossible had it not been for his married status.

> When Jesus came into Peter's home, He saw his mother-in-law lying sick in bed with a fever. (Matt. 8:14)

The Apostle Paul even used Peter as an example of the fact that Christian ministers have the liberty to get married:

> Do we not have a right to take along a believing wife, even as the rest of the apostles and the brothers of the Lord and Cephas? (1 Cor. 9:5)

Interestingly, *Cephas* is Peter's Aramaic name. In First Corinthians 9:5 Paul is speaking of Peter, that indeed he had "a believing wife."

The Catholic Church had attempted to hide the Bible from the people for centuries, because they knew that the things that they were teaching went directly against the Word of God. Following the Reformation, however, this was no longer possible.

For one thing, they discovered that is possible both to serve God and to be married—as Luther himself put into practice. Luther married a former Catholic nun named Katharina von Bora.

The Ultimate Sacrifice

As a result of their efforts, in many cases the Reformers paid the ultimate sacrifice to give us the great gifts that they gave us. Yes, many of them were martyred for their faith.

One of Luther's contemporaries was William Tyndale (1494—1536), who shared his passion to put the Bible in the language of the people—in this case the English people.

He created a Bible version, which is named after him—taken directly from the Hebrew and Greek. For that, he paid with his life. His dying prayer was, "Lord, open the king of England's eyes." And he was willing to die for this righteous cause.

Many of these Reformers suffered greatly for what they gave us—things that many of us simply take for granted. God has advanced truth in His church at the cost of great sacrifice.

Rejoice!

As this chapter has explained, the contributions of the Protestant Reformers are of inestimable value. Such contributions include a return to literal interpretation and the authority of the Scriptures, the articulation of the five *solas* and an emphasis upon the priesthood of all believers—which, in turn, positively impacted the accessibility of Bible translations as well as literacy standards, the basis of the American system of governance and the rejection of ministerial celibacy. Therefore, as we look back at the Protestant Reformers, who in some cases paid the ultimate price of martyrdom to advance their cause, our mindset ought to be one of rejoicing in these men—and what God did through them.

CHAPTER 5

The Reformers' Incomplete Revolution

As much as the Reformation offers us things for which we ought to thank God, there are also some negative things of which we must be aware.

Sometimes there is a tendency to whitewash this history because we so appreciate the good things that the Reformers did. We may even think of them as deserving to be placed on a pedestal. But, of course, the only one who belongs on that pedestal is the Lord Jesus Christ Himself.

There were errors in the minds of the Reformers that they never corrected. It would be historically naïve to think that the Protestant Reformers fixed 1,000 years of bad teaching in such a short period of time. Now, they corrected it in many key areas, such as the *solas*. Yet other subjects were left untouched. Many Protestant churches today, following their heritage, are still operating by a deficient belief system in some areas.

Many Reformed churches are Protestant in some ways, but continue to be Roman Catholic in others. Here is the key: The weakness of Reformed theology is that people took the progress made by the Reformers and presumed that there was no further progress to be made. They took that progress and froze it into creeds and confessions, such as the Westminster Confession, which became the authority.

Luther believed in *sola Scriptura*. Therefore, such a non-scriptural authority base goes against the very principles for which the Reformers stood. And what you have in Reformed thought is a hybrid, a mixture, of Protestantism and Roman Catholicism. They are Protestant soteriologically, but remain Alexandrian, Origenistic, Augustinian or Roman Catholic in terms of eschatology. And it is difficult for those inside the system to question this, because the creeds and confessions have, in fact, become their authority. And, yet, this is tragic because your eschatology will control your philosophy of ecclesiology.

This is a side of the Protestant Reformation that most people will not bring up, or even think about.

God had to raise up other people to further correct the damage done at Alexandria, Egypt—which the Reformers left uncorrected. We will study that important part of church history in depth later in the book.

The Danger of Fossilizing Tradition

Do you remember when the children of Israel came out of Egypt and went to Mount Sinai? As they were passing through the Transjordan region, serpents began to bite the people. They complained to Moses, and he took it to the Lord. Here is what Moses did next, at God's direction:

> And Moses made a bronze serpent and set it on the standard; and it came about, that if a serpent bit any man, when he looked to the bronze serpent, he lived. (Num. 21:9)

In His conversation with Nicodemus in John 3, Jesus used that as an object lesson for salvation:

> As Moses lifted up the serpent in the wilderness, even so must the Son of Man be lifted up; so that whoever believes will in Him have eternal life. (John 3:14-15)

Simply looking to Christ, metaphorically—by way of faith—will save you, not from a snake bite, but from the greatest poisonous disease which has ever infected the human race, which is the disease of sin, which affects all of us.

But whatever happened to that bronze serpent?

Second Kings 18:4 tells us what happened to it 800 years after it was first made, just before the Babylonian deportation—in the days of King Hezekiah, who fought much idolatry in the land of Israel:

> He removed the high places and broke down the *sacred* pillars and cut down the Asherah. He also broke in pieces the bronze serpent that Moses had made, for until those days the sons of Israel burned incense to it; and it was called Nehushtan.

The children of Israel took something that God had used and turned it into an idol. This happens in almost every tradition. Eventually every movement will fossilize and worship the very instrument or person that God originally used—perhaps even to condemn idolatry.

My contention is that this is what has happened to a large degree with the Protestant Reformers. They are elevated almost to the level of the saints who are worshiped within Roman Catholicism. I believe that the Reformers themselves would be embarrassed by this misplaced obeisance. But this is the tendency of human nature. And it leads to our propensity to look away from seeing anything negative in them.

The proper way to understand the Protestant Reformation is to adhere to the principles for which the Reformers stood, rather than to put the Reformers themselves on a pedestal where they, frankly, do not belong.

Almost every denomination or tradition has some relic of idolatry, because people are so appreciative of the good that a leader has done that they have the inclination to elevate that person to a place where he or she does not belong.

In the eyes of some people, we must not ever challenge the Reformers or Reformation theology.

Actually, I think that the principles that the Protestant Reformation gave to us provide the basis by which anything may be challenged. The whole point is *sola Scriptura*.

Remember what God said to Joshua in Joshua 1:2:

> *Moses My servant is dead*; now therefore arise, cross this Jordan, you and all this people, to the land which I am giving to them, to the sons of Israel. (italics added)

Why did God have to call the next generation's attention to Moses' death? It is because of the tendency to venerate human leaders—especially those like Moses who have led for 40 years.

May I say respectfully—Martin Luther, like Moses, is also dead. John Calvin is also dead.

We appreciate many heroes of the past, and what they have given us, but they are dead. They are no longer the issue. The issue is the principles that they gave to us.

These Reformers were people—human beings, just like Peter, whom we have studied.

God used Peter. Jesus called him "blessed" in Matthew 16:17, and there was not a more pivotal leader in the early church than him (cf. Acts 1—10).

But Jesus had to call Peter "Satan" in Matthew 16:23. Peter was just a man with a sin nature. We do not elevate or venerate Peter. In fact, he himself would not want that.

We have seen the Reformers' positive contributions. Now we must consider their incomplete revolution—and, consequently, the incomplete state of Reformed theology today, and why God had to raise up other people to use the same literal interpretive method that the Reformers themselves gave to us.

The Reformers had a wonderful method—but they did not apply it comprehensively. There were reasons for that. But other people had to take their hermeneutical methodology and apply it to the entire Bible.

The Protestant Reformers knocked over a big domino. But there were other dominoes still to follow.

There are some negative things to understand about the Protestant Reformers, and once you realize that you understand why God raised up others outside of the Reformed tradition to restore truths to the church that the allegorical method of interpretation had subverted. These later characters began to take the Reformers' literal method of interpretation and apply it to other parts of the Bible, which the Reformers had left untouched.

What the Reformers Did and Did Not Do

Protology

One of the things that I really appreciate about the Protestant Reformers is their view of Genesis and origins. As far as I can tell, the Reformers took Genesis 1 to 11 in its literal sense. Now, this was before 1859 and the publication of Charles Darwin's *Origin of the Species*.[63] Following the publication of that book, many Christians began to be intimidated by what scientists were saying about the age of the Earth. They wanted to be relevant, and came up with many beliefs about Genesis that cannot be substantiated by God's Word—such as the day-age theory, the gap theory, the local flood theory, progressive creationism and theistic evolution.

They accepted the secular understanding of the fossil record and de-emphasized the flood. These are all compromises within the evangelical

---

63 Charles Darwin, *On the Origin of the Species by Means of Natural Selection, or the Preservation of the Favoured Races in the Struggle for Life* (NY: Appleton, 1859).

church. The book that reversed this course is *The Genesis Flood*[64]—by Dr. Henry Morris, the fully credentialed scientist, and Dr. John Whitcomb, the theologian and fully credentialed Hebrew scholar. They gave up on the notion of rewriting Genesis and decided to challenge the secular scientists on the basis of the authority of the Word of God. They challenged evolution and other unbiblical interpretations of history.

Indeed, Whitcomb and Morris gave us a different way of interpreting these things, by which we could maintain the integrity of Genesis 1 to 11 and interpret scientific findings in light of the literal interpretation of those chapters.

Back in the pre-Darwinian 16th century, the Reformers were not under such intense pressure to rewrite the book of Genesis. What you will find, then, is that they took their literal method of interpretation that they used to reclaim the five *solas* and applied it very well to protology—the doctrine or study of beginnings. You do not find them advocating any compromise views regarding creationism.

Notice what Martin Luther stated:

> We know from Moses that *the world was not in existence before 6,000 years ago*. . . . He calls "a spade a spade," i.e., *he employs the term "day" and "evening" without allegory, just as we customarily do* . . . we assert that *Moses spoke in the literal sense, not allegorically or figuratively, i.e., that the world, with all its creatures, was created within six days*, as the words read. If we do not comprehend the reason for this, let us remain pupils and leave the job of the teacher to the Holy Spirit.[65] (italics added)

Notice Luther's emphasis on 24-hour creation days and a young earth. Again, this is one of the things that I appreciate about the Protestant

64 John Whitcomb and Henry Morris, *The Genesis Flood: The Biblical Record and Its Scientific Implications* (Philippsburg, NJ: Presbyterian & Reformed Publishing, 1961).

65 Martin Luther, "Lectures on Genesis 1–5," in *Luther's Works*, ed. Jaroslav Pelikan (St. Louis: Concordia, 1958), pp. 3, 6.

Reformers. John Calvin speaks similarly:

> And they will not refrain from guffaws when they are informed that but little more than *five thousand years have passed since the creation of the universe*. . . . Must we pass over in silence the creation of the universe? No! God's truth is so powerful, both in this respect and in every other, that it has nothing to fear from the evil speaking of wicked men. [66] (italics added)

For Luther and Calvin, Genesis 1 to 11 contains literal truth to be clearly understood and believed.

Consider the description of the flood in Genesis 7:19-23. It shows clearly that the flood was global:

> The water prevailed more and more upon the earth, so that *all the high mountains everywhere under the heavens were covered*. The water prevailed fifteen cubits higher, and the mountains were covered. *All flesh* that moved on the earth *perished*, birds and cattle and beasts and *every* swarming thing that swarms upon the earth, and *all* mankind; of all that was on the dry land, *all* in whose nostrils was the breath of the spirit of life, died. Thus He blotted out *every* living thing that was upon the face of the land, from man to animals to creeping things and to birds of the sky, and they were blotted out from the earth; and *only* Noah was left, together with those that were with him in the ark. (italics added)

It is very clear that the flood waters covered the whole Earth. But post-Darwin, people thought it must take billions of years to explain the fossil record. Therefore, evangelicals began to view the explanation of the fossil record in terms of a sudden, worldwide catastrophe, such as the global flood, as untenable. Consequently, evangelicals began to syncretize the findings of modern-day *science* with Scripture.

One tool that they used in this endeavor was the local flood theory, which

---

66 John Calvin, *Institutes of the Christian Religion*, III, xxi, 4.

teaches that the flood never covered the entire world, but rather just covered a local area in Mesopotamia. This hermeneutical maneuver allows interpreters to still hold to some remnants of the Bible but also to embrace worldly philosophy by explaining the fossil record through gradual accumulation over billions of years as opposed to a sudden, catastrophic deluge. Thus, as 1 Timothy 6:20 (KJV) speaks about people advocating "science falsely so called"—which is just philosophy masquerading as science—evangelicals began trying to mix the Bible with the words of scientists. Since evolution is taught in our public schools as an unquestionable fact, this approach is very easily adopted. What we must do instead, however, is to hold to the integrity of the Bible and go out and challenge the unbiblical notions of the scientific world on that basis.

Notice what Calvin said about the flood:

> And the flood was forty days, etc. Moses conspicuously insists on this fact, in order to show that the *whole world* was immersed in the waters.[67] (italics added)

Thus, these quotes from Luther and Calvin demonstrate that the Protestant Reformers did not follow the syncretistic approach that is popular among many so-called *evangelicals* today, but rather stood on the integrity and authority of God's Word in the foundational area of protology.

Selective Literalism

This next point, however, relates to something that the Reformers did not do nearly as well.

We actually find that they were very selective with their literal interpretation. Unfortunately, they still carried allegorization with them into some other areas of Bible interpretation—including ecclesiology (the doctrine of the church) and eschatology (the doctrine of the end times).

Roy Zuck states:

67 John Calvin, *Genesis*, 1554 (Edinburgh, UK: Banner of Truth, 1984), p. 272.

> Though Luther vehemently opposed the allegorizing of Scripture, he too occasionally allegorized. For instance, he stated that Noah's Ark is an allegory of the Church. For Luther, Bible interpretation is to be centered in Christ. Rather than allegorizing the Old Testament, he saw Christ frequently in the Old Testament, often beyond what is legitimately provided for in proper interpretation.[68]

Luther basically employed a Christocentric hermeneutic—wanting to see Jesus everywhere in the Bible. The problem with this is that you begin to find Jesus in places where He is not described—unless you apply allegorization.

In general, the Reformers used literal interpretation effectively to rescue the church in certain important areas, but they did not go far enough with it. They were very selective in its application.

Failure to Deal in Depth with Eschatology

Eschatology is the study of the end. The Reformers largely ignored this subject.

Calvin wrote a commentary on every single New Testament book except Second and Third John and Revelation. Zuck explains:

> ...he wrote commentaries on every book of the Bible except 14 Old Testament books and 3 New Testament books. Those books are Judges, Ruth, 1 and 2 Samuel, 1 and 2 Kings, 1 and 2 Chronicles, Ezra, Nehemiah, Esther, Proverbs, Ecclesiastes, Song of Songs, 2 and 3 John, and Revelation.[69]

One of the reasons that people like Calvin so much is that he comments on nearly every single verse in the Bible. He is a voluminous writer, speaker

68 Roy B. Zuck, *Basic Bible Interpretation: A Practical Guide to Discovering Biblical Truth* (Colorado Springs, CO: Victor, 1991), p. 45.

69 Ibid., 47.

and preacher—but leaves us with the impression that the book of Revelation cannot be understood.

The Reformers took an aggressive stand on protology, but they really did not deal with eschatological issues.

In fact, Luther wrote some amazing words in the preface of the Bible translation that he produced. This is what he said regarding the book of Revelation:

> I miss more than one thing in this book, and this makes me hold it to be neither apostolic nor prophetic. . . . I think of it almost as I do of the Fourth Book of Esdras, and can in no way detect that the Holy Spirit produced it. . . . It is just the same as if we did not have it, and there are many far better books for us to keep. . . . Finally, let everyone think of it as his own spirit gives him to. My spirit cannot fit itself into this book. There is one sufficient reason for me not to think highly of it—Christ is not taught or known in it; but to teach Christ is the thing which an apostle is bound, above all else, to do, as He says in Acts 1, "Ye shall be my witnesses." Therefore I stick to the books which give me Christ, clearly and purely.[70]

Apparently, Luther rejected the book of Revelation as being the product of Divine inspiration. Here, Luther makes an analogy between Revelation and uninspired writings. This statement captures that negative attitude that both he and Calvin had toward end-time prophecy.

In fact, in 1545, Luther printed the book of Revelation, along with Hebrews, James and Jude, as an appendix to the New Testament.

---

70 Martin Luther, *Preface to the New Testament*, 1522. Available at http://www.godrules.net/library/luther/NEW1luther_f8.htm; Internet; accessed 18 November 2017.

Retaining Augustinian Amillennialism

The Reformers kept Augustine's doctrine that there is no literal 1,000-year kingdom of Jesus Christ upon the Earth.

When will we have this kingdom? When we have the king—Jesus Christ, seated on David's throne and reigning from Jerusalem. But this cannot happen until Jesus returns (cf. Rev. 19:11-16). That is the essence of premillennialism.

Why does this matter so much? The answer is that it affects what the Christian and the church should be doing now, in the present. Many churches today are trying to establish the kingdom. That can lead to de-emphasizing the gospel and focusing instead on social issues—trying to fix the problems in the world.

Premillennialists recognize that this will not work, because we cannot have kingdom conditions until the king is present.

Now, we should be involved in holding back or slowing down the tide of evil. But the majority of our time should be spent trying to reach and teach—evangelize and disciple.

Amillennialism began through the influence of Alexandria, Egypt, and dominated the church throughout the Middle Ages. But the Reformers did not apply their literal method of interpretation to this issue. Instead, sadly, they simply carried the false teaching of amillennialism over into the Reformation.

Remember, it was Augustine who crystallized this doctrine into a written treatise—*The City of God*—which influenced the church all throughout the Middle Ages, and continues to do so today. He wrote:

> The saints reign with Christ during the same thousand years, understood in the same way, that is, of the time of His first coming. . . . Therefore the Church even now is the kingdom of Christ, and the kingdom of heaven. Accordingly, even now His saints reign with Him.[71]

71 Augustine, *The City of God*, trans., Marcus Dods (NY: Random House, 1950), Book XX, chap. 9, pp. 725-26.

This was a watershed statement by a very influential man. Notice what Calvin wrote later:

> Augustine is so wholly with me, that if I wished to write a confession of my faith, I could do so with all fullness and satisfaction to myself out of his writings.[72]

Calvin is acknowledging his dependence on the theology of Augustine. Thus, Reformed churches today are a hybrid—Protestant in certain areas, but still Roman Catholic in other areas. The great weakness of the Reformed tradition is that they assumed that there was no more progress to be made, and froze their progress in terms of creeds—which became the authority in place of the Scriptures.

We can make application to this situation from Joshua 13:1:

> Now Joshua was old *and* advanced in years when the LORD said to him, "You are old *and* advanced in years, and very much of the land remains to be possessed."

There is still much more Roman Catholic thinking, carried over by the Reformers, that needs to be challenged. And the Reformation gave us the tools whereby these doctrines could be reclaimed. We must use these tools consistently from Genesis to Revelation.

Calvin also said this regarding the millennial kingdom and premillennialism:

> But Satan has not only befuddled men's senses to make them bury with the corpses the memory of resurrection; he has also attempted to corrupt this part of the doctrine with various falsifications.... Now their fiction is too childish either to need or to be worth a refutation. And the Apocalypse, from which they undoubtedly drew a pretext for their error, does not support them.

72 John Calvin, "A Treatise on the Eternal Predestination of God," in *John Calvin, Calvin's Calvinism*, trans. Henry Cole (Grandville, MI: Reformed Free Publishing Association, 1987), p. 38.

> For the number "one thousand" [Rev. 20:4] does not apply to the eternal blessedness of the church but only to the various disturbances that awaited the church, while still toiling on earth. . . . Those who assign the children of God a thousand years in which to enjoy the inheritance of the life to come do not realize how much reproach they are casting upon Christ and his Kingdom.[73]

Calvin first published his *Institutes* at age 26. Certainly he was a brilliant man, but his young age should give us at least a bit of pause. Calvin said a lot of great things, and he said a lot of things that were flatly wrong. We dare not elevate his writings to the level of Scripture, because that is dangerous and moves into the area of idolatry. His writing here comes off as being very prideful.

Here he is telling us that we are in the kingdom right now in the present, and that placing it in the future is a *childish* fantasy. In fact, Calvin notes here that those who place a literal kingdom into the future are actually *casting reproach upon* Christ's alleged current spiritual kingdom as He now reigns (within the Reformed understanding) through the church. This type of kingdom-now thinking comes directly from Augustine, as we have seen.

Denial of Israel's Future Prophetic Role

What was the attitude of the Protestant Reformers toward the Jews? Anti-Semitism, the idea that the Jews are Christ-killers and a cursed race, dominated Middle Ages thinking.

It is true that the leadership of first-century Israel was instrumental in the death of Christ—breaking every rule of evidence that they had and rushing Him through the justice system. But we could also blame the Romans (e.g., Matt. 20:19; John 19:11). Moreover, Jesus died for all of us—and in that sense all of us killed Him (cf. John 3:16). We cannot blame it all on the Jews.

73 John Calvin, *Institutes of the Christian Religion*, III, xxv, p. 5.

What developed out of this anti-Semitism is the concept of replacement theology—the doctrine that the church has permanently replaced Israel in the plan and program of God and is, even now, functioning as the kingdom of God. Most of Christendom, by way of denominational affiliation in the United States of America, and also worldwide, holds to replacement theology.

What does that mean in practice? First, prophetic subjects are often neglected completely. But when they are taught, the idea set forth is that all of Israel's promises and blessings have been transferred to the church, which they call the *New Israel*—even though the word *Israel* refers to the physical descendants of Abraham, Isaac and Jacob all 73 times that it is found in the New Testament. The Jews themselves then become the cursed race, and the curses found in the Old Testament remain with them. The blessings promised to Israel, now supposedly given to the church, must be wildly spiritualized, since they are earthly in nature.

The Reformers never used their literal method of interpretation to correct the church in the area of replacement theology. We often find them writing about the idea that the Jews have been cut off completely—there is no future for Israel in their thinking. The only good thing that can happen to a Jew is that he or she can be saved and become part of the church. While Jewish conversion in the present church age is indeed wonderful, it rules out the hope of the future kingdom for national Israel. Calvin exemplifies this replacement theology line of thinking when he writes:

> But by this public call, the Gentiles were not only made equal to the Jews, but seemed to be substituted into their place, as if the Jews had been dead.[74]

The Protestant Reformers remained Catholic in the areas of ecclesiology and eschatology.

74 John Calvin, *Institutes of the Christian Religion*, II, xi, 12.

Consider also this comment from Calvin's sermon on 2 Samuel 24:24, when he declares:

> Now the Jews are cut off like rotten limbs. We have taken their place.[75]

Now, is Israel broken off from God's olive tree, as he says? Yes, but Paul tells us in Roman 11 that this breaking off is only temporary:

> But if some of the branches were broken off, and you, being a wild olive, were grafted in among them and became partaker with them of the rich root of the olive tree, do not be arrogant toward the branches; but if you are arrogant, *remember that* it is not you who supports the root, but the root *supports* you. You will say then, "Branches were broken off so that I might be grafted in." Quite right, they were broken off for their unbelief, but you stand by your faith. Do not be conceited, but fear; for if God did not spare the natural branches, He will not spare you, either. Behold then the kindness and severity of God; to those who fell, severity, but to you, God's kindness, if you continue in His kindness; otherwise you also will be cut off. And they also, if they do not continue in their unbelief, will be grafted in, for God is able to graft them in again. For if you were cut off from what is by nature a wild olive tree, and were grafted contrary to nature into a cultivated olive tree, how much more will these who are the natural *branches* be grafted into their own olive tree? (Rom. 11:17-24)

See, if God can do the greater miracle of grafting the *wild*, unnatural branches (Gentiles) into the olive tree, then certainly He can do the lesser miracle of grafting the *natural branches* back into their own tree. And Paul cautions the Gentiles here against becoming *arrogant* regarding their standing. John Calvin became very arrogant toward the natural branches, did he not?

According to replacement theology, the Gentiles are not just partakers

75 John Calvin, *Supplementa Calviniana*, I, 766, 12f; quoted in Herman J. Selderhuis, ed., *The Calvin Handbook* (Grand Rapids, MI: Eerdmans, 2009), p, 145.

of God's blessings—we are taker-overs. We have inherited all of Israel's promises, but leave the curses for the Jewish people. This is a carry-over from Augustine and the Middle Ages.

Notice again that Calvin also declares Israel to be "cut off from everything," adding haughtily, "and we have succeeded them in their place."[76]

As we have seen, the Apostle Paul leaves no room for arrogance on this subject. Yet I am seeing arrogance here in Calvin's writings.

Notice his comments on this verse from Isaiah, which speaks of the restoration of Israel in the end times:

> The wilderness and the desert will be glad,
> And the Arabah will rejoice and blossom;
> Like the crocus. (Isa. 35:1)

Calvin says:

> This passage is explained in various ways. I pass by the *dreams of the Jews*, who *apply all passages of this kind to the temporal reign of the Messiah*, which they have contrived by *their own imagination*. . . . I willingly view this passage as referring to Judea, and afterwards *to other parts of the world*. . . . Let us now see when this prophecy was fulfilled, or shall be fulfilled. The Lord began some kind of restoration when he brought his people out of Babylon: but that was only a foretaste, and, therefore, I have no hesitation in saying that this passage, as well as others of a similar kind, must *refer to the kingdom of Christ*; and in no other light could it be viewed, if we compare it with other prophecies.[77] (italics added)

Calvin here calls literal interpretation a *dream*—a mere fantasy. He dismisses that method of literal interpretation—even though he made his

---

76 John Calvin, *Supplementa Calviniana*, II, 36, 28f; Sermon on Isa. 14:2; quoted in Selderhuis, *The Calvin Handbook*, p. 145.

77 John Calvin, Commentary on Isaiah 35:1. (2015). *Commentary on the Book of the Prophet Isaiah*. Bellingham, WA: Logos Bible Software.

most important contributions by advocating for it in other areas. But he refuses to apply it to this passage. Consequently, Calvin denies Israel's future millennial role.

Consider this prophecy of Israel's restoration in her kingdom—never to be uprooted again—from the book of Amos:

> "Behold, days are coming," declares the LORD,
> "When the plowman will overtake the reaper
> And the treader of grapes him who sows seed;
> When the mountains will drip sweet wine
> And all the hills will be dissolved." (Amos 9:13)

How did Calvin handle that passage?

> Here the Prophet describes the felicity which shall be under the reign of Christ: and we know that whenever the Prophets set forth promises of a happy and prosperous state to God's people, they adopt *metaphorical expressions*, and say, that abundance of all good things shall flow, that there shall be the most fruitful produce, that provisions shall be bountifully supplied; for they *accommodated* their mode of speaking to the notions of *that ancient people*; it is therefore no wonder if they sometimes *speak to them as to children*. At the same time, the Spirit under these figurative expressions declares, that *the kingdom of Christ* shall in every way be happy and blessed, or that *the Church of God*, which means *the same thing*, shall be blessed, when Christ shall begin to reign.[78] (italics added)

Metaphorical expressions? Literal construction as a mere Divine accommodation to *children*? Notice again how Calvin indicates that these prophecies really apply to the present reigning church and how national Israel is consequently written out of her future kingdom role. Where is the man who stood heroically for literal interpretation? Who is the real John Calvin? I do

78 John Calvin, Commentary on Amos 9:13. (2015). *Commentary on the Twelve Minor Prophets.* Bellingham, WA: Logos Bible Software.

not want Calvin the allegorizer—I want Calvin the literalist!

The word *accommodated* is nothing but a fancy term indicating that God here is *lying*. But remember that it is impossible for God to lie:

> ... in the hope of eternal life, which God, who cannot lie, promised long ages ago. (Tit. 1:2)
>
> ... so that by two unchangeable things in which it is impossible for God to lie, we who have taken refuge would have strong encouragement to take hold of the hope set before us. (Heb. 6:18)
>
> God is not a man, that He should lie,
> Nor a son of man, that He should repent;
> Has He said, and will He not do it?
> Or has He spoken, and will He not make it good? (Num. 23:19)

And what about this phrase: "speak to them as to children"? Is God speaking in childish terms to childish people who cannot understand real interpretation? Is this just a fantasy for people who do not know better than to believe in a literal kingdom? Calvin is saying that it only looks literal to you because you are childish, and God is speaking to you in childish terms.

Calvin calls these "figurative expressions" and says the church "means the same thing" as the kingdom.

Let us examine his comments on one more passage:

> In that day His feet will stand on the Mount of Olives, which is in front of Jerusalem on the east; and the Mount of Olives will be split in its middle from east to west by a very large valley, so that half of the mountain will move toward the north and the other half toward the south. (Zech. 14:4)

How do we interpret this? It means that Jesus will return and stand on the Mount of Olives, and it will split in half. But Calvin develops a soteriological meaning that is not at all self-evident from this passage. He is not performing exegesis when he states:

> For as we are dull and entangled in earthly thoughts, our minds can hardly rise up to heaven, though the Lord with a clear voice invites us to himself. The Prophet then, in order to aid our weakness, adds a vivid representation, as though God stood before their eyes. Stand, he says, shall his feet on the mount of Olives. He does not here promise a miracle, such as *even the ignorant might conceive to be literal*; nor does he do this in what follows, when he says, The mount shall be rent . . . half . . . to the east and half to the west. This has never happened, that mount has never been rent: but as the Prophet could not, under those grievous trials, which might have overwhelmed the minds of the godly a hundred times, have extolled the power of God . . . without employing a highly figurative language, *he therefore accommodates himself, as I have said, to the capacity of our flesh.*[79] (italics added)

Now he is calling literal interpreters *ignorant*. And he again uses "accommodates . . . to the capacity of our flesh." This type of language is an excuse for dismissing the clear meaning of the passage. And he says, "This has never happened." The reason for that is simple—it is a prophecy of things yet future.

Sadly, such a minimization of Israel's future, national millennial role carried over into the various movements and institutions begun by the Reformers in the wake of the Protestant Reformation.

Showers stated in summary:

> The Lutheran, Reformed, and Anglican Reformers rejected Premillennialism as being "Jewish opinions." They maintained the Amillennial view which the Roman Catholic Church had adopted from Augustine.[80]

Thus, the Reformers did not make a clean break with Roman Catholicism in the area of eschatology.

---

79 John Calvin, Commentary on Zechariah 14:4. (2015). *Commentary on the Twelve Minor Prophets.* Bellingham, WA: Logos Bible Software.

80 Renald Showers and John Ankerberg, *The Most Asked Prophecy Questions* (Chattanooga, TN: ATRI, 2000), pp. 328.

Barry Horner has written:

> The inheritance from the Augustinian tradition that modern Europe received, notwithstanding the opposition of Melanchthon and others to Luther's excesses, resulted in a continuance of an eschatology that upheld the essentially anti-Judiac thesis, namely, the transference of blessings, formerly promised to Israel, to the Christian church for its fulfillment. . . . On a much larger scale the reformed movement maintained its allegiance to Augustinian eschatology, which essentially found authoritative expression in the writings of Francis Turretin (1623–1687) who studied at Calvin's academy in Geneva and later taught there for 30 years. His monumental *Institutes of Elenctic Theology* became the epitome of reformed doctrine. Not surprisingly, his quotations of Augustine are copious, even far exceeding references to Calvin. Consequently, Turretin's eschatology is almost predictable. . . . Of course such a mass incorporation into the church is to the exclusion of any perpetuation of Jewish identity. In classic Augustinian fashion, there is token recognition of Jewish individuality for a time, though any form of Jewish restoration was considered to be a gross form of chiliasm. Turretin's *Institutes* became the central textbook for systematic theology in American Ivy League colleges during the later half of the 18th century. It is not surprising that the early theologians of Princeton Theological Seminary highly esteemed this most influential legacy, and of course its eschatology.[81]

On May 14, 1948, replacement theology met its match when Israel came back to life as a nation in its homeland. Replacement theologians then had to come up with a way to explain away the rebirth and existence of the modern state of Israel. Some have even gone so far in their antagonism as to engage in formal boycotts of the state of Israel.

---

81 Barry Horner, *Future Israel: Why Christian Anti-Judaism Must Be Challenged*, ed. E. Ray Clendenen, NAC Stuides in Bible & Theology (Nashville, TN: Baker, 2007), pp. 155-60.

Pope and Papacy Viewed as Antichrist and Babylon

One of the ideas that you will find coming from the Protestant Reformers is the charge that the pope is the antichrist. Luther discovered that this preached well to those who did not appreciate many of the abuses of the Roman Catholic Church. The question is: Is this what the Bible really teaches?

Personally, I think that there are enough bad things within Roman Catholicism and its theology that we do not need to label them as the antichrist in order to effectively denounce them. Nor is that a sufficient basis to allow us to assign meaning to Biblical prophecy at our own whim.

Furthermore, a careful study of eschatological passages does not yield the conclusion that the city or system of Babylon is Rome or the pope.

Luther and Calvin did not exercise the same care and precision when studying eschatology as they did when studying Romans and Galatians. We could really call what they did in the area of eschatology *newspaper exegesis.*

Babylon in Revelation 17 and 18 refers, literally, to Babylon. Babylon is in the east, in Mesopotamia. Rome is in the west.

Luther took much of his interpretation from Revelation 17:9-10:

> Here is the mind which has wisdom. The seven heads are *seven mountains on which the woman sits*, and they are seven kings; five have fallen, one is, the other has not yet come; and when he comes, he must remain a little while. (italics added)

Thus, Luther believed that this passage refers to Rome, which is universally known as *the city on seven hills*. However, here the text itself tells us that the *seven mountains* represent *seven kings*. It is not a reference to Rome.

We know from Daniel that *king* and *kingdom* may be used interchangeably. The basis for this interpretation comes from Daniel 2:37-38:

> You, O *king*, are the *king of kings*, to whom the God of heaven

> has given the *kingdom*, the power, the strength and the glory; and wherever the sons of men dwell, *or* the beasts of the field, or the birds of the sky, He has given *them* into your hand and has caused you to rule over them all. You are the head of gold. (italics added in first two lines)

Thus, I believe that Revelation 17:9-10 refers to seven kingdoms that persecuted the nation of Israel. On this basis, I believe that Revelation 17:9-10 has nothing to do with the seven hills of Rome.

Also, in Revelation 17:3 we find:

> I saw a woman sitting on a scarlet beast, full of blasphemous names, having seven heads and ten horns.

The woman is named "BABYLON" (Rev. 17:5). The beast upon which she sits controls these seven mountains. Thus, the seven mountains belong to the antichrist's system rather than the woman named Babylon. The seven hills are not speaking about the Roman Catholic Church. Nor can both the woman named *Babylon* and the beast with the seven hills be Rome, for the beast destroys the woman in v. 16. How can Rome destroy Rome?

Yet, despite these exegetical problems, note Luther's interpretation of the Antichrist's destruction as predicted in 2 Thessalonians 2:8:

> No man can believe what an abomination *the papacy* is. A Christian does not have to be of low intelligence, either, to recognize it. God himself must deride him in the hellish fire, and our Lord Jesus Christ, St. Paul says in II Thessalonians 2, "will slay him with the breath of his mouth and destroy him by his glorious coming." I only deride, with my own weak derision, so that those who now live and those who will come after us should know what I have thought of *the pope, the damned antichrist*, and so that whoever wishes to be a Christian may be warned against such an abomination.[82] (italics added)

82 Martin Luther, "Against the Roman Papacy, an Institution of the Devil," in *Luther's Works*, ed. Eric.

Calvin wrote similarly:

> However, when we categorically deny to *the papists* the title of the church, we do not for this reason impugn the existence of churches among them. Rather, we are only contending about the true and lawful constitution of the church, required in the communion not only of the sacraments (which are the signs of profession) but also especially of doctrine. Daniel (Dan. 9:27) and Paul (2 Thess. 2:4) foretold that *Antichrist* would sit in the Temple of God. With us, it is *the Roman pontiff* we make the leader and standard bearer of that wicked and abominable kingdom. The fact that his seat is placed in the Temple of God signifies that his reign was not to be such as to wipe out either the name of Christ or of the church. From this it therefore is evident that we by no means deny that the churches under his tyranny remain churches. But these he has profaned by his sacrilegious impiety, afflicted by his inhuman domination, corrupted and well-nigh killed by his evil and deadly doctrines, which are like poisoned drinks. In them Christ lies hidden, half buried, the gospel overthrown, piety scattered, the worship of God nearly wiped out. In them, briefly, everything is so confused that there we see the face of *Babylon* rather than that of the Holy City of God.[83] (italics added)

This method of labeling the pope as the antichrist was wildly popular with the people, but it also demonstrates the lack of care that the Reformers used in dealing with Bible prophecy. There are still many more corrections to be made in eschatology because the Reformers handed us ideas that were not based on the literal interpretation of Scripture.

W. Gritsch (Philadelphia, PA: Fortress Press, 1966), pp. 273-74.

83 John Calvin, *Institutes*, IV, ii, 12.

Retention of Roman Catholic Vestiges

The Reformers also dragged other vestiges of Roman Catholicism with them into their new Protestant and Reformed churches. People have been taught that the Reformers made a clean break with Roman Catholicism. But it would be naïve to think that way. They brought much errant baggage with them.

We do this as well—especially those of us who have had a lifetime of thinking wrongly before coming to believe in Christ. Our minds are not instantly purified. That is why Romans 12:1-2 tells us:

> Therefore I urge you, brethren, by the mercies of God, to present your bodies a living and holy sacrifice, acceptable to God, *which is* your spiritual service of worship. And do not be conformed to this world, but be transformed by the renewing of your mind, so that you may prove what the will of God is, that which is good and acceptable and perfect.

New Christians must submit to this process of mental renewal through the perpetual intake of God's Word and discipleship that leads them through "the whole purpose of God" (Acts 20:27). Otherwise the mind will continue to think along the same paths that it always has.

The verse that I like to use to illustrate this is Daniel 7:12:

> As for the rest of the beasts, their dominion was taken away, but an extension of life was granted to them for an appointed period of time.

This is talking about the fact that the kingdoms in Daniel, such as Babylon, continued to live on spiritually in the subsequent political systems that followed them. In other words, although Persia conquered Babylon (Dan. 5), Daniel here predicted that Babylon would not be annihilated but rather would live on culturally within the Persian empire. Similarly, although

Greece conquered Persia, Daniel here predicted that both Babylon and Persia would not be annihilated but rather would live on culturally within the Grecian empire. Furthermore, although Rome conquered Greece, Daniel here predicted that Babylon, Persia and Greece would not be annihilated but rather would live on culturally within the Roman empire. In fact, historians will tell you that Rome conquered Greece politically, but Greece conquered Rome culturally. Rome kept the Greek language, deities and many other aspects of its society.

This is an illustration of what the Protestant Reformation accomplished. Roman Catholicism continued to live on in the minds of the Reformers and their spiritual descendants.

In fact, one of the things that we must understand about Luther and Calvin is that they never wanted to leave Rome at all. It was never their intention. Protestantism was the work of the Holy Spirit, but humanly speaking it was an unintended consequence.

Luther and Calvin were both trained to be monks or priests and wanted to stay Catholic. The reason they finally left is that they experienced *the right foot of fellowship*—they were kicked out. So they were forced to begin new churches, which was contrary to their initial intention.

After Luther nailed his 95 theses to the door of the Castle Church in Wittenberg, Germany, on Oct. 31, 1517, he was shocked more than anyone when people began to call him a heretic. All that he wanted to do was to begin a discussion about certain points that bothered him—particularly the manipulation of the sheep by the priesthood. He merely wanted to reform the existing Roman Catholic Church from within.

Thus, it is not shocking at all that these men dragged much of Roman Catholicism along with them into their newfound Protestantism.

Infant Baptism

One of these things was the practice of infant baptism.

But how does baptism work in the Bible?

> Then Philip opened his mouth, and beginning from this Scripture he preached Jesus to him. As they went along the road they came to some water; and the eunuch *said, "Look! Water! What prevents me from being baptized?" [And Philip said, "If you believe with all your heart, you may." And he answered and said, "I believe that Jesus Christ is the Son of God."] And he ordered the chariot to stop; and they both went down into the water, Philip as well as the eunuch, and he baptized him. When they came up out of the water, the Spirit of the Lord snatched Philip away; and the eunuch no longer saw him, but went on his way rejoicing. (Act. 8:35-39)

Notice that the Biblical pattern is that the gospel is first shared with someone, who believes the gospel and is saved, and then the next logical step after that is water baptism. Water baptism saves no one, but rather it is merely an outward confession of an inward reality. This pattern is repeated numerous times throughout the book of Acts (cf. Acts 8:12; 10:43-48; 16:14-15, 30-34; 18:8). Water baptism always follows a conversion through faith alone (cf. Matt. 28:19).

The Bible never teaches that you should baptize an infant. The simple reason is that there is no way to validate that an infant has believed. You must wait until a person achieves some level of maturity, so the person can give an authentic testimony of faith in Christ.

The Roman Catholic Church had been in the business of baptizing infants—a non-Biblical tradition. Luther dragged this into Protestantism without correcting it. Concerning Luther, McGrath notes how he believed that:

> … such sacraments could generate faith; and hence baptism could generate faith of an infant.[84]

Where did Luther get such an idea? It does not come from the Bible, but rather from the long line of tradition that had been handed to him.

Consubstantiation

One of the other things that the Protestant Reformers dragged with them into their new church movement was a variation of the Roman view of the Lord's Supper.

The Roman Catholic Church taught transubstantiation. This is the concept that to partake of communion is literally to eat the physical body of Jesus Christ and to drink His physical blood.

That means that Christ is being re-crucified at every single Mass! That immediately runs afoul of the book of Hebrews, which tells us that the crucifixion is a singular event which could only happen one time (cf. Heb. 9:28). In fact, Transubstantiation also sounds much like cannibalism.

Luther takes this unbiblical doctrine and puts a lighter spin on it. Caner explains:

> Luther denied the doctrine of Transubstantiation, rejecting any molecular change of the elements. Consubstantiation, a term never employed by Luther, is used to explain his view that the body and blood are present 'in, with, and under' the bread and wine.[85]

The idea here is that when the elements of communion are served, Jesus is there in a special way. In fact, His presence is so unique during that sacrament that He is not there in that way at other times.

---

84 Alister E. McGrath, *Reformation Thought: An Introduction* (Grand Rapids: Baker, 1995), p. 179.

85 Emir Caner, "Balthasar Hubmaier and His Theological Participation in the Reformation: Ecclesiology and Soteriology," *Faith and Mission* 21, no. 1 (2003): 42.

Perhaps we can see how this teaching would be attractive on several levels. The problem is that there is no verse of Scripture that teaches it. The Bible does not teach that Jesus is present during communion in a way that He is not present during the rest of the church service.

We instead believe the memorial view of communion. Jesus discusses this in Luke 22:19-20:

> And when He had taken *some* bread *and* given thanks, He broke it and gave it to them, saying, "This is My body which is given for you; do this *in remembrance* of Me." And in the same way *He took* the cup after they had eaten, saying, "This cup which is poured out for you is the new covenant in My blood." (italics added in the third line)

We participate in this ordinance "in remembrance of" what Jesus did on the cross. It is a memory device, triggered by the bread and the cup.

God works through symbols to remind people of what He has done (cf. Gen. 9:8-17). The bread reminds us of Christ's body, and the cup reminds us of His blood. We are reminded of the fact that salvation is not free, but was paid for by Christ at the greatest cost. Yet we are not actually partaking in His physical body and blood, nor even saying that He is present in some mystical way.

To be fair, Luther did not have time to correct all of these problems. Yet, by dragging these doctrines into Protestantism, he had the effect of causing great harm in Christ's church.

This is what you find the Protestant Reformers doing over and over again.

The Ramifications of Teaching That the Church is the Kingdom of God on the Earth

We have seen previously how Augustine refined the belief that the church is the kingdom of God upon the Earth. If you believe that, it has implications and ramifications ecclesiologically and even politically. Augustine, for instance, had no problem using the force of law to punish people who disagreed with him theologically.

After all, if you believe that the church is the kingdom of God on the Earth—here to take over society—it is a logical outflow of that idea that the church should grab the reins of power and coerce people to become Christians.

Augustine advised Marcellinus, an African governor, to punish the Donatists (a Christian sect who objected to certain church practices) as quoted here:

> . . . not by stretching them on the rack, nor by furrowing their flesh with iron claws, nor by scorching them with flames, but by beating them with rods.[86]

Therefore, the organized, visible church was hated throughout the Dark Ages—because it practiced things such as this.

Recall Calvin's concession concerning his own dependence upon the theology of Augustine, when he admitted:

> Augustine is so wholly with me, that if I wished to write a confession of my faith, I could do so with all fullness and satisfaction to myself out of his writings.[87]

86 "Augustine: Advice to Marcellinus on the Punishment of Donatists, 412," in J. Stevenson, ed., *Creeds, Councils, and Controversies: Documents Illustrating the History of the Church, AD 337–461* (London: SPCK, 1966), p. 213.

87 John Calvin, "A Treatise on the Eternal Predestination of God," in *John Calvin, Calvin's Calvinism*, trans. Henry Cole (Grandville, MI: Reformed Free Publishing Association, 1987), p. 38.

Calvin is here acknowledging his dependence on the theology of Augustine. Thus, it is no great surprise to discover that in matters of church discipline Calvin imitated Augustine's totalitarian style of government. Calvin, carrying these practices with him into the Protestant Reformation, took political control of a city, Geneva, Switzerland, and also put theological opponents to death.[88] That is the logical outworking of kingdom-now theology.

Calvin used the Mosaic Law as the basis for punishing people who were theologically out of line. However, what does the Psalmist say about the Mosaic Law?

> He declares His words to Jacob,
> His statutes and His ordinances to Israel.
> He has not dealt thus with any nation;
> And as for His ordinances, they have not known them.
> Praise the LORD! (Ps. 147:19-20)

The Psalmist is very clear that the law was given only to Israel. Also, remember that you cannot just take a part of the Old Testament law and implement only that:

> For whoever keeps the whole law and yet stumbles in one *point*, he has become guilty of all. (Js. 2:10)

If you are under the Mosaic Law in any way, then you are bound by the whole system—not just its moral implications, but also its ceremonial and punitive implications. You cannot just pick and choose the parts of the Mosaic Law that you want to follow. The New Testament is clear that believers today are not under the law of Moses, but are rather under "the law of Christ" (Gal. 6:2; cf. Rom. 6:14), which is given in the New Testament revelation.

Yet Calvin did not operate this way. Rather, he acted as follows:

---

88 Dave Hunt, *What Love Is This? Calvinism's Misrepresentation of God*, 4th ed. (Bend, OR: Berean Call, 2013), pp. 67-87.

> ... Calvin sought to reconstruct a society through the imposition of the Mosaic Law, "which he tried to imitate as much as possible in his new Christian republic in Geneva."[89]

This led to totalitarianism in Geneva. The *Encyclopaedia Judaica* refers to Calvin's "despotic theocratic regime in Geneva."[90] Another scholar offers this appraisal:

> A measure of legalism became apparent in Geneva, as the consistory put the lives of church members under continuous review and applied discipline to offenders. Church attendance was compulsory. Eating fish on Fridays was forbidden, as were attendance at theaters, dancing, cardplaying, and criticism of pastors. All heretical teaching was deemed subversive and subject to penalties under criminal law. Flagrant infractions could lead to banishment, imprisonment, and in extreme cases death. Judicial torture was common procedure.[91]

This is the dark side of the Reformation—an Augustinian mindset that continues on into Protestantism. We know immediately that it is outside of God's will to coerce anyone to become a Christian using the force of law. God has created all people "in His own image" (Gen. 1:27) and people retain this image-bearing status even in their fallen state (cf. Gen. 9:6; Jas. 3:9). The fall has merely effaced this reality rather than completely erasing it. Part of this status involves the capacity for choice. Therefore, any form of coercion applied to people to induce a Christian conversion is not the voice of the Holy Spirit, but rather epitomizes a tyrannical form of legalism.

The dark storm cloud that hovers over Calvin is the death of Michael Servetus, who held unorthodox views of the Trinity. One source records:

---

89 "Calvin, John," *Encyclopedia Judaica* (Jerusalem: Keter Publishing, 1971), Vol. 5, p. 66.

90 Ibid., p. 67.

91 James Edward McGoldrick, "Introducing John Calvin: The Reformer's Preparation," *Reformation and Revival* 10, no. 4 (2001): 21.

> "The execution of Servetus is the greatest blot on Calvin's life" and reveals "that vindictive streak which sometimes disgraced the character of the Reformer."[92]

And Servetus was not the only one. Dave Hunt notes:

> In February of 1555, Calvin's supporters gained the absolute majority on the council [in Geneva]. On May 16, there was an attempted uprising because Calvin had excluded certain libertarian civic officials from the Lord's Supper. Leaders of the rebellion who fled to Bern were sentenced to death in abstentia. Four who failed to escape were beheaded, quartered, and their body parts hung in strategic locations as a warning. Evoking the phrase "henchmen of Satan," which he had used years earlier against the Anabaptists, Calvin justified this barbarity by saying, "Those who do not correct evil when they can do so and their office requires it are guilty of it." From 1554 until his death in 1564, "no one any longer dared oppose the Reformer openly."[93]

Sadly, there are many people in Christendom—on the left and the right—that are trying to do similar things today. We must remember that this is the devil's world—and only Jesus can take that world back over when He returns. Until then, all kingdom now *take-over* social experiments will ultimately end in tragic results. Yet, Augustinian and Roman Catholic kingdom now theology continues to live and breathe amongst the Protestant Reformers and their spiritual lineage.

Anti-Semitism

I have given the Reformers their rightful due, but history is history. As we have noted, Anti-Semitism began to transpire early on in church

92 Lewis Lupton, *A History of the Geneva Bible* (London: Olive Tree, 1969), Vol. 2, pp. 23–24.

93 Dave Hunt, "Calvinism Denied," in *Debating Calvinism: Five Points, Two Views*, ed. Dave Hunt and James White (Sisters, OR: Multnomah, 2004), pp. 23-24.

history and continued unabated throughout the Middle Ages.[94] Therefore, the Reformers did not invent anti-Semitism, but they also did not correct it.

Not long after nailing his "95 Theses" to the Castle Church door in Wittenberg, Germany (1517), and following his excommunication (1521), still early in his career, in 1523, Luther wrote a great book called *Jesus Was Born a Jew*. It was very pro-Jewish. Here is an excerpt of it:

> If I had been a Jew and had seen such dolts and blockheads govern and teach the Christian faith, I would sooner have become a hog than a Christian. They have dealt with the Jews as if they were dogs rather than human beings; they have done little else than deride them and seize their property. When they baptize them they show them nothing of Christian doctrine or life, but only subject them to popishness and monkery. . . . If the apostles, who also were Jews, had dealt with us Gentiles as we Gentiles deal with the Jews, there would never have been a Christian among the Gentiles. . . .[95]

Luther went on to say:

> When we are inclined to boast of our position we should remember that we are but Gentiles, while the Jews are of the lineage of Christ. We are aliens and in-laws; they are blood relatives, cousins, and brothers of our Lord. Therefore, if one is to boast of flesh and blood, the Jews are actually nearer to Christ than we are. . . . If we really want to help them, we must be guided in our dealings with them not by papal law but by the law of Christian love. We must receive them cordially, and permit them to trade and work with us, that they may have occasion and opportunity to associate with us, hear our Christian teaching, and witness our Christian life. If some of them should prove stiff-necked, what of it? After all, we ourselves are not all good Christians either.[96]

94 Michael L. Brown, *Our Hands Are Stained with Blood: The Tragic Story of the "Church" and the Jewish People* (Shippensburg, PA: Destiny Image, 1992), pp. 7–17.

95 Martin Luther, *Jesus Was Born a Jew*, 1523. Available at https://www.uni-due.de/collcart/es/sem/s6/txt09_1.htm; Internet; accessed 18 November 2017.

96 Ibid.

Luther is confessing that Christians' witness toward the Jews had been less than Biblical and had alienated them from Christianity.

But 20 years later in 1543, Luther wrote another book called *Of the Jews and Their Lies*. Luther had labored to retrieve salvation by grace alone and held it out to the Jewish people, and got no response—so his attitude began to change back to the attitude that many held during the Dark Ages. Here are some excerpts from this horrible book:

> First, their synagogues should be set on fire. . . . Secondly, their homes should likewise be broken down and destroyed. . . . Thirdly, they should be deprived of their prayer books and Talmud. . . .[97]

This is despicable anti-Semitism. He goes on to say:

> Fourthly, their rabbis must be forbidden under threat of death to teach any more. . . . Fifthly, passport and traveling privileges should be absolutely forbidden to the Jews. . . . Sixthly, they ought to be stopped from usury. . . .[98]
>
> Seventhly, let the young and strong Jews and Jewesses be given the flail, the ax, the hoe, the spade, the distaff, and spindle, and let them earn their bread by the sweat of their noses. . . . We ought to drive the rascally lazy bones out of our system. . . .[99]
>
> . . . Therefore away with them. . . . To sum up, dear princes and nobles who have Jews in your domains, if this advice of mine does not suit you, then find a better one so that you and we may all be free of this insufferable devilish burden—the Jews.[100]

In that same year, Luther also wrote a pamphlet called *Of the Unknowable Name and the Generations of the Messiah*. In it, he calls the Jews "little devils."

97 Martin Luther, *The Jews and Their Lies* (1852; reprint, York, SC: Liberty Bell, 2004), pp. 37-38, 53-54.

98 Ibid., pp. 38-40, 54-55.

99 Ibid., pp. 42-43.

100 Luther, *The Jews and Their Lies*; quoted in Brown, *Our Hands Are Stained with Blood*, pp. 14–15.

Then in 1546, he preached his final four sermons in Eisleben, calling the Jews the enemies of Christianity, and calling for them to be kicked out of the country.[101]

There are many who seek to look the other way or whitewash history to suppress Martin Luther's later anti-Semitic tendencies. However, this is difficult to do because Lutheran leaders themselves have issued their own public apology for the anti-Semitic outbursts of their spiritual forebear. The Lutheran World Federation presented the following statement in 1984:

> We Lutherans take our name and much of our understanding of Christianity from Martin Luther. But we cannot accept or condone the violent verbal attacks that the Reformer made against the Jews.... The sins of Luther's anti-Jewish remarks, the violence of his attacks on the Jews, must be acknowledged with deep distress. And all occasions for similar sin in the present or the future must be removed from our churches.... Lutherans of today refuse to be bound by all of Luther's utterances on the Jews.[102]

There is also a school of thought that indicates that what Luther said laid the groundwork for Nazi Germany. As we have seen, he did not invent anti-Semitism, but he did carry it over. Concerning Luther's latter remarks, the *Encyclopaedia Judaica* states: "Short of the Auschwitz oven and the extermination, the whole Nazi holocaust is pre-outlined here."[103] Lucy Dawidowicz similarly states: "A line of anti-Semitic descent from Martin Luther to Adolf Hitler is easy to draw. Both Luther and Hitler were obsessed by a demonologized universe inhabited by the Jews."[104]

---

101 Olivier J. Melnick, *End-Times Antisemitism: A New Chapter in the Longest Hatred* (Tustin, CA: Hope For Today Publications, 2017), pp. 88-92.

102 "Interreligious Documents & Statements: Luther, Lutheranism, and the Jews," https://www.ccjr.us/dialogika-resources/documents-and-statements/interreligious/759-lwfijcic1983; Internet; accessed 25 November 2017.

103 "Luther, Martin," *Encyclopedia Judaica*, Vol. 8, p. 693.

104 Lucy S. Dawidowicz, *The War Against the Jews: 1933–1945* (NY: Holt, Rinehart, and Winston, 1975), p. 23.

Olivier J. Melnick writes:

> In 1543, when the Jewish community didn't meet his expectations, Luther published the book *Of the Jews and Their Lies*, where his description of the Jewish people is so venomous that Hitler was quoted saying that he was just finishing up what Luther started.... As a matter of fact, many scholars and historians believe that Luther's view of the Jews had a profound effect on Germans for centuries to come and also had a serious influence on Hitler's ideology and implementing the final solution to the Jewish question. The connection between Luther and Hitler is not difficult to make.[105]

And Thomas Ice notes:

> ...Hitler was not alone in his irrational desire to murder Jews, it was embedded in the German, Austrian, and Eastern European nations. The original source for such anti-Semitism goes back to the common experience of all of Europe's medieval Roman Catholic Jew-hatred. Most of the people throughout Europe did not have to be taught by Hitler or the Nazis to hate the Jews, it was endemic in their culture for hundreds of years. When the Nazis crystalized their anti-Semitism into murdering the Jews as a virtue, they already had a willing mass of people ready to join their crusade. After all, Hitler quoted the founder of the Reformation three times in *Mein Kampf* and called Martin Luther one of the greatest Christians in all of history. It is not surprising (for the most part) the German clergy were great Hitler enthusiasts since almost all of them were liberal and held to replacement theology.[106]

The only meaningful force standing in the way of anti-Semitism, even in our country today, comes from Bible-believing and reading Christians who see in the Scripture a Divine future for national Israel.

So how do we look at someone like Martin Luther? We look at him just

---

105 Melnick, *End-Times Antisemitism*, pp. 89, 92.

106 Thomas Ice, "Yad Vashem and the Holocaust," http://www.pre-trib.org/articles/view/yad-vashem-and-the-holocaust; Internet; accessed 26 October 2017.

like we do the Apostle Peter—a man capable of both great highs and great lows (cf. Matt. 16:13-23). Christians, believe it or not, have the capability of saying both great things and things that are horrific or even demonically energized. This is true because of the fact that Christians possess two natures—including the old nature.

Satan especially desires to tempt Christian leaders that God has used in great ways—to get them to fall and thus nullify the effect that they have had for good. After all, we must remember that the Reformers were just men—vessels of clay.

And we can see these same anti-Semitic tendencies in John Calvin, who stated:

> But here he [the rabbi] not only betrays his ignorance, but his utter stupidity, since God so blinded the whole people that they were like restive dogs. I have had much conversation with many Jews: I have never seen either a drop of piety or a grain of truth or ingenuousness—nay, I have never found common sense in any Jew. But this fellow, who seems so sharp and ingenious, displays his own impudence to his great disgrace.[107]

Calvin repeatedly refers to the Jews as "profane unholy sacrilegious dogs,"[108] describing them as "a barbarous nation"[109] and "the people of Israel rejected by God."[110]

What did the Apostle Paul say about the Jews? He specifically noted that the Gentile believers are not to become *arrogant* toward the unbelieving Jews (cf. Rom. 11:18). Then he added:

---

107 John Calvin, Commentary on Daniel 2:44. (2015). *Commentary on the Book of the Prophet Daniel.* Bellingham, WA: Logos Bible Software.

108 John Calvin, *Ioannis Calvini opera quae supersunt Omnia,* 50, 307; Sermon on Gal. 1:6–8; quoted in Herman J. Selderhuis, ed., *The Calvin Handbook* (Grand Rapids, MI: Eerdmans, 2009), p. 145.

109 John Calvin, *Supplementa Calviniana,* V, 145, 10; Sermon on Mic. 40b–11; quoted in, p. 145. Selderhuis, *The Calvin Handbook*

110 John Calvin, *Ioannis Calvini opera quae supersunt Omnia,* 27, 6; Sermon on Deut. 10:1–8; quoted in Selderhuis, *The Calvin Handbook*, p, 145.

> From the standpoint of the gospel they are enemies for your sake, but from the standpoint of *God's* choice they are beloved for the sake of the fathers; for the gifts and the calling of God are irrevocable. (Rom. 11:28-29)

We must view the Jewish people through the lens of the Abrahamic Covenant—and determine to bring the gospel to them in a loving and meaningful way. Ultimately, the Reformers failed to do so.

Sadly, the Reformers fell down on following these Pauline injunctions at all, instead adopting an attitude of pride toward the unbelieving Jews. They neglected to show love to them in spite of their present state of unbelief.

A Realistic Picture

The Reformers did not focus on the whole picture—likely due to fatigue and to their expending of so much energy to concentrate on the five *solas*. Yes, some of them paid for their convictions with their own lives. We can look back upon them with gratitude, but we must not put them on pedestals. We recognize that what they did successfully was to provide the right method by which future generations could continue to reform the church. This is accomplished through the consistent application of their interpretive approach. In other areas, they fell far short and provide merely a negative example.

The Protestant Reformation continues today—because the Reformers left much work untouched. This history is here to teach about both the good and the bad of the Protestant Refomration, and we must learn from it.

CHAPTER 6

Reformed Theology Today

The Reformation which the Protestant Reformers introduced was partial, at best. Much work has been left undone. What then is the state of Reformed theology today?

The churches that owe their direct spiritual lineage to the Protestant Reformers carry on today with an incomplete theology. Unless we understand this, we will not understand why God continued to reform the church through others—outside of the Reformed tradition.

The error of Reformed theology is, first of all, that it erroneously assumes that there was no further progress to be made following the Reformers—no more ground to conquer. The Reformers' advances were wonderful indeed, yet how naïve it would be to think that no further progress was necessary or possible.

This thinking must be an error because of a precept that we find in Daniel 12:4 and 9:

> "But as for you, Daniel, conceal these words and seal up the book until the end of time; many will go back and forth, and knowledge will increase."
>
> He said, "Go *your way*, Daniel, for *these* words are concealed and sealed up until the end time."

God is speaking to Daniel through the angel Gabriel. He predicted that right up until the end of the age there would always be further ground to be conquered. Therefore, the Protestant Reformation could not have been the end of all Biblical truth.

Daniel is very specific in his prophecy here that—as the human race draws ever closer to the end of the age—more truth would be forthcoming.

Now, the canon of Scripture was shut with the writing of the book of Revelation by the Apostle John, so this is not referring to the giving of more new revelation (cf. Jude 3; Rev. 22:18-19). Rather, it speaks of new understanding. Truths which have always been there in the text will be made known in a new and fresh way, at an increasing rate, as we move closer to the end of the age—particularly in the area of prophecy.

Since John completed the book of Revelation at the end of the first century, there has been no more *progressive revelation*. However, there is the *progressive illumination* of the Scriptures that we already possess.

This means that we can actually know things that Luther, Tyndale, Zwingli and Calvin could not know. This is not necessarily because we are any smarter or more spiritual than any of them, or because we have an additional book of the Bible that they did not have. Rather, it is simply because we are living later in history.

Also, we must remember that the Holy Spirit continued to reform the church even after these reformers died—and He does so still today. If the Lord tarries, the next generation will rightfully see things in the Scriptures that we today do not see. They will have a deeper understanding that we do not yet have. To use Daniel's term, such information is becoming gradually but progressively *unsealed.*

Consider also that statement from Daniel 12:4, which reads, "Many will go back and forth, and knowledge will increase."

These words are often misinterpreted to refer to things in the last days such as air travel, cruises and, of course, the Internet. However, we must compare this verse to another that uses a similar Hebrew construction—Amos 8:12:

> People will stagger from sea to sea
> And from the north even to the east;
> They will go to and fro to seek the word of the LORD,
> But they will not find *it*.

What is the purpose of this movement "to and fro," or "back and forth" as Daniel describes it? It is "to seek the word of the LORD."

So what Daniel is describing is people reading the Bible as the world moves toward the end times. Going "to and fro" is reading, not traveling. They will see things in the Bible that the sages of the past were unable to find. This is progressive illumination.

Sir Isaac Newton and the Time of the End

Did you know that Sir Isaac Newton (1642—1727) was a devout Christian? In fact, he is considered to be the founder of modern science and the man who discovered the law of gravity. Yet he spent more time studying the Bible than he did science. Secularists criticize him for this, thinking he could have made even greater scientific discoveries if he had just devoted himself to that task in a greater way and spent less time in Bible study. But the reality of the situation is that Newton's knowledge of the Bible gave him an incentive to study science.

Newton's belief in a Creator God led him to believe that the universe was governed by laws that the Creator Himself had established. This led him to study the natural world just as aggressively as he studied the Scriptures.

Most people are also unaware that Newton wrote Bible commentaries on the books of Daniel and Revelation. He was a tremendous student of the end times, and he made this statement about Daniel's prophecies:

> About the time of the end, a body of men will be raised up who will turn their attention to the Prophecies, and insist upon their literal interpretation, in the midst of much clamor and opposition.[111]

111 Isaac Newton; quoted in Nathaniel West, *The Thousand Years in Both Testaments* (Fincastle, VA: Scripture Truth, 1889), p. 462.

Newton's comment sheds light upon Daniel 12:4 and 9, and it is consistent with the idea of *progressive illumination*.

The attitude of many Reformed theologians, on the other hand, is that if you cannot find a concept in the writings of Luther or Calvin, then it is not Biblically true.

Frozen Progress

What Reformed theology has done, in essence, is to take the progress of the Reformers and freeze it into creeds and confessions. Then they assume that the final statement of truth is found in these creeds and confessions.

One of the most famous such documents is the Westminster Confession. It states in one place regarding eschatology:

> 1. At the last day shall be a general resurrection of the dead both of the just and of the unjust. 2. All found alive shall be immediately changed. 3. Immediately after the resurrection shall follow the general and final judgment of all angels and men, good and bad. 4. That the date of this day and hour is purposely kept secret by God.[112]

We see in this statement the error of reductionism—taking a complex subject and oversimplifying it. They have one general resurrection at the end, for everyone. I actually find this statement to be woefully inadequate and incomplete. The Bible presents a much bigger picture regarding eschatology, which is far more intricate and complex than the one offered by the Westminster Confession.

112 *Westminster Confession of Faith*. Chapters 32 and 33; "Larger Catechism," Questions 87–89. Available at http://www.ligonier.org/learn/articles/westminster-confession-faith/; Internet; accessed 28 November 2017.

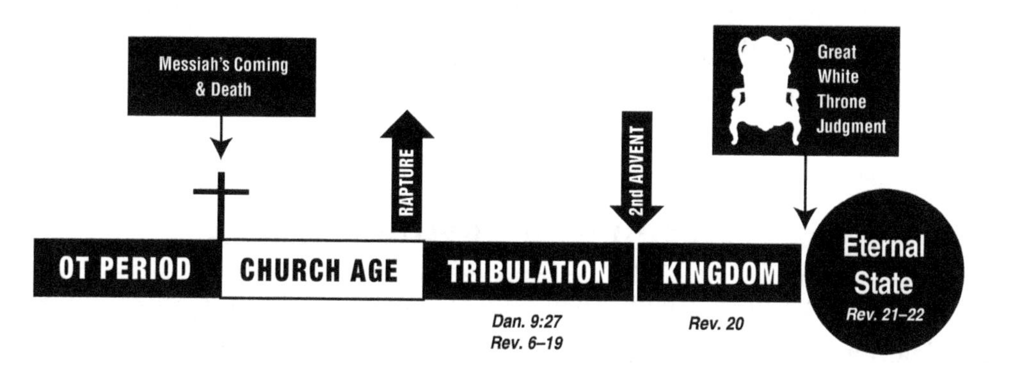

For one thing, there are different resurrections for different groups at different times. These fit within and around the events such as the rapture, the seven-year tribulation, the 1,000-year earthly kingdom of Christ and the great white throne judgment. But to find all of these things, you must leave the Westminster Confession and turn your attention to the pages of Scripture, using the same method of literal interpretation that the Protestant Reformers used to rescue the church through the five *solas*.

But in Reformed circles, the authority becomes the Westminster Confession. What happens, then, is that you interpret Scripture through the lens of the Westminster Confession. It has become the authority. Many of the branches of the descendants of the Reformation do this same thing with the various creeds and confessions that they follow in their particular groups.

The problem is that this defies Luther's emphasis on *sola Scriptura*.

Our authority must be, and remain, the Bible. What we teach must be Biblical. It does not matter if Luther or Calvin understood a concept or not, or which creed or confession included it; if it is Biblical, then we must teach it. If it is not Biblical, then we must not.

Jeremy Edmondson states:

> The goal of the Reformation was to point Christianity back to the Scriptures. The noble intentions of the Reformers called for the Bible as the supreme authority for believers everywhere. For

> this we rejoice! But if the Reformation and its resulting creeds are exalted to the standard of measuring orthodoxy, does it not defeat the very purpose for which it was intended?[113]

Keeping Augustine Alive

Furthermore, Augustinian amillennialism has been fossilized into Reformed theology. The spiritualizing of the kingdom, the teaching that it is here now, was never corrected by the Protestant Reformers.

To use a different metaphor, Augustinian amillennialism—which was brought into existence thanks to the allegorical hermeneutics from Origen at Alexandria—lives and breathes and is alive and well within Reformed theology.

Showers states it this way:

> The Lutheran, Reformed, and Anglican Reformers rejected Premillennialism as being "Jewish opinions." They maintained the Amillennial view which the Roman Catholic Church had adopted from Augustine.[114]

Reformed churches today are a hybrid. They are Protestant—in certain areas, particularly the *solas*. But they remain Roman Catholic in other areas, including the very important subjects of the doctrine of the church and the doctrine of the end times. This is why we see Christian denominations of the Reformed tradition doing activities such as economic boycotts against the Jewish people and the land of Israel instead of blessing them. Their theology is naturally working its way out.

Barry Horner states:

> The inheritance from the Augustinian tradition that modern

---

113 Jeremy Edmondson, "Returning to Scripture as Our Sole Authority," in *Free Grace Theology: 5 Ways It Magnifies the Gospel*, ed. et al. Charlie C. Bing (Allen, TX: Bold Grace, 2016), p. 3.

114 Renald Showers and John Ankerberg, *The Most Asked Prophecy Questions* (Chattanooga, TN: ATRI, 2000), p. 328.

> Europe received, notwithstanding the opposition of Melanchthon and others to Luther's excesses, resulted in a continuance of an eschatology that upheld the essentially anti-Judiac thesis, namely, the transference of blessings, formerly promised to Israel, to the Christian church for its fulfillment. . . . On a much larger scale the reformed movement maintained its allegiance to Augustinian eschatology, which essentially found authoritative expression in the writings of Francis Turretin (1623–1687) who studied at Calvin's academy in Geneva and later taught there for 30 years. His monumental *Institutes of Elenctic Theology* became the epitome of reformed doctrine. Not surprisingly, his quotations of Augustine are copious, even far exceeding references to Calvin. Consequently, Turretin's eschatology is almost predictable. . . . Of course such a mass incorporation into the church is to the exclusion of any perpetuation of Jewish identity. In classic Augustinian fashion, there is token recognition of Jewish individuality for a time, though any form of Jewish restoration was considered to be a gross form of chiliasm. Turretin's *Institutes* became the central textbook for systematic theology in American Ivy League colleges during the later half of the 18th century. It is not surprising that the early theologians of Princeton Theological Seminary highly esteemed this most influential legacy, and of course its eschatology.[115]

This is the very reason why Lewis Sperry Chafer started Dallas Theological Seminary in the 1920s, because he was displeased with the things that were coming out of Princeton Seminary.

Reformed theology today includes the ideas of covenant theology, or covenantalism.

Distinctives of Covenantalism

What is covenant theology? Here are some important distinctives:

115 Barry E. Horner, *Future Israel: Why Christian Anti-Judaism Must Be Challenged*, ed. E. Ray Clendenen, NAC Studies in Bible & Theology (Nashville, TN: Baker, 2007), pp. 155-60.

1. A system of interpreting the Scriptures on the basis of two covenants: the covenant of works and the covenant of grace. Some add the covenant of redemption.
2. The importance of grace. In every age, believers are always saved by grace.
3. God's primary purpose on Earth is redemptive.
4. Partial allegorical system of hermeneutics.

The only point here that is agreeable is point two. There are some things within covenant or Reformed theology—even within replacement theology—that are true. But this does not make the entire system true.

Point three above is not true. God's overarching purpose in human history, including in His work of redemption, is to bring glory to Himself.

If your definition of what God is doing is too narrow, then there are parts of the Bible that cannot be explained. For instance, if God's primary purpose on Earth is redemptive, then how do we also explain the fall of the angels—and the fact that the plan of salvation is not open to the fallen angels? We must have an overarching rubric that captures all of the Biblical data. Short of having that, you will begin interpreting the Bible allegorically whenever it appears necessary to make the Scripture fit your preexisting system. This is what we see in Reformed theology.

Regarding the three covenants of covenant theology, I also disagree. I think that dispensationalists, with our emphasis on the *Biblical* covenants, are the real covenant theologians.

The covenants of covenant theology are not discovered exegetically in the Bible. Rather, they are merely inferred from the Scriptures. These covenants are:

1. The Covenant of Works – God entered into a covenant with Adam as the federal head of the human race. God promised eternal life for obedience and eternal death for disobedience.

2. Covenant of Redemption – This is a covenant made between God the Father and God the Son in eternity past in which they covenanted together for the redemption of the human race.
3. Covenant of Grace – This is a covenant made by God with the elect in which He provides salvation to the elect sinner.

This covenant of grace becomes a lens through which adherents of covenant theology read the entire Bible. Because of this, certain parts of the Bible must be dehistoricized, de-literalized and soteriologized.

For instance, the covenant theologian looks at the promise of the land tract given to Abraham, and tells us that this land tract is not land on planet Earth—but rather that it will be in heaven. They must do the same thing with promises made to Abraham and his descendants regarding a future, physical kingdom.

In some cases, this leads to ignoring major passages or books of the Bible—especially the book of Revelation.

Reformed theology is not liberalism, because its teachers do not allegorize the entire Bible. They take the gospels and epistles literally, for instance. But if they were to take the allegorical method, which they use to interpret prophecy, and apply it to the whole Bible, they would become full-blown liberals. If they did not interpret some concepts—such as the five *solas*—literally, they would not even be orthodox.

Yet, as important as the covenants of grace and works are to the entire system of covenant theology, no less of an authority on Reformed Theology than Charles Hodge has stated concerning the covenant of works:

> This statement does *not* rest upon any express declaration of the Scriptures . . . [and] although the word covenant [as in works] is *not used* in Genesis, and does not elsewhere, in any clear passage, occur in reference to the transaction there recorded. . . it is *plain* that the Bible does represent the arrangement made with Adam

> as a truly federal transaction.[116] (italics added)

Dispensationalist Charles Ryrie notes this glaring omission, when he says:

> The covenant theologian *never* finds in the Bible the terms *Covenant of Works* and *Covenant of Grace*."[117]
>
> The point is . . . simply to show that they are deductions, not inductions, from Scripture. The existence of the covenants is not found by an inductive examination of passages."[118]
>
> But there is *not one* reference from Scripture in the several sections that deal directly with the establishment of the covenant of grace or its characteristics. There are references concerning the blessings of salvation but none to support the covenant of grace. What is missing is rather significant and revealing.[119]

These covenants are not found in the Bible, as Hodge admits here. They are not exegetically derived. Rather, they are merely manufactured, theological covenants.

Zechariah 14:4

Now, here is a passage that some would allegorize. But is it obvious from the verse that it should be taken in a merely metaphorical sense?

> In that day His feet will stand on the Mount of Olives, which is in front of Jerusalem on the east; and the Mount of Olives will be split in its middle from east to west by a very large valley, so that half of the mountain will move toward the north and the other half toward the south. (Zech. 14:4)

This verse talks literally about the coming of Jesus Christ. But seen

116 Charles Hodge. *Systematic Theology*. Vol 2, p. 117 (2015). Bellingham, WA: Logos Bible Software.

117 Charles C. Ryrie, *Dispensationalism Today* (Chicago: Moody, 1965), p. 184.

118 Ibid., p. 185.

119 Charles C. Ryrie, *Dispensationalism* (Chicago: Moody, 1995), p. 190.

through the covenant of grace, the covenant theologian takes this verse to refer to the redemption of the individual—and to Christ piercing the believer's heart.

David Reagan makes a great statement about this:

> Let me give you a classic example of spiritualization taken from the writings of a theologian by the name of Loraine Boettner. It has to do with his interpretation of Zechariah 14:1-9. That passage says that in the end times Jerusalem will be surrounded by enemy forces and will be ready to fall to them when the Lord will suddenly return to the Mount of Olives. When His feet touch the Mount, it will split down the middle. The Lord will then speak a supernatural word that will instantly destroy all the enemy forces. And on that day, the Lord will become King over all the earth. In his commentary on this passage, Boettner completely spiritualized it. He argued that the Mount of Olives stands for the human heart. The enemy forces symbolize the evil in this world that surrounds and attacks the heart. The Lord's return represents what happens when a person accepts Jesus as Lord and Savior. Thus, when Jesus comes into a person's heart, their heart (the Mount of Olives) splits in contrition, and all the evil influences in the person's life are defeated, and Jesus becomes king of that person's heart. That's what I call an exercise in imagination![120]

Yet, such unrestrained allegorization is very common in Reformed theology.

Global Events Yet to Occur

Another view that is promoted in Reformed circles is preterism, from the Latin word for *past*. This is the idea that the whole book of Revelation, with perhaps a few exceptions, has already taken place and been fulfilled in the past—especially with the events of A.D. 70. But think what you have

120 David Reagan, "The Beginning and the Ending," http://christinprophecy.org/articles/the-beginning-and-the-ending/; Internet; accessed 19 April 2017, p. 1.

to do to the Apocalypse's global language to have it fulfilled in a local event of the past.

Recent preterist commentators and advocates include R.C. Sproul, N.T. Wright, Scott Hahn, J. Massyngbaerde Ford, David Chilton, Hank Hanegraaff and Kenneth Gentry.

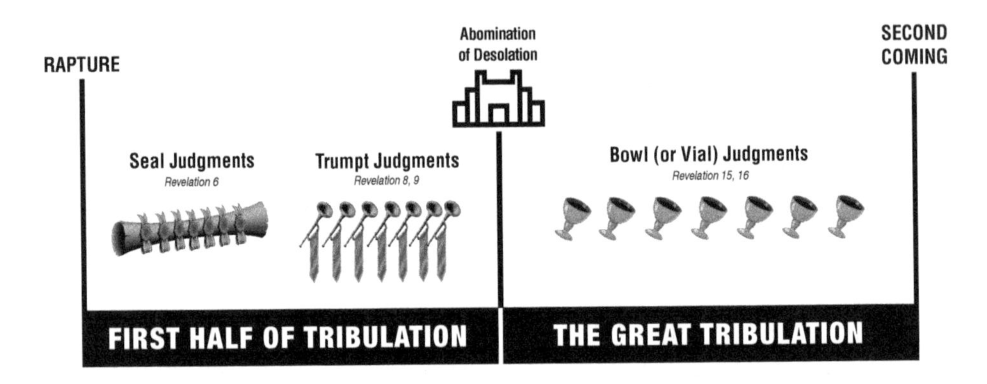

Revelation Describes Future Events

1. Half of the world's population destroyed (Rev. 6:8; 9:15)
2. Sea turns to blood (Rev. 16:3)
3. Greatest earthquake in history (Rev. 16:18)
4. "The great city" that reigns over the entire Earth (Rev. 17:18)

How can we fit all of these global events into the local events of A.D. 70? You cannot do so without employing an allegorical interpretation.

Preterist Kenneth Gentry states:

> . . . the preterist view does understand Revelation's prophecies as strongly reflecting actual historical events in John's near future, though they are set in apocalyptic drama and clothed in poetic hyperbole.[121]

121 Kenneth L. Gentry, "A Preterist View of Revelation," in *Four Views on the Book of Revelation*, ed. C. Marvin Pate (Grand Rapids: Zondervan, 1998), p. 38.

R.C. Sproul similarly writes:

> Russell and Calvin agree that the language employed in biblical prophecy is not always cold and logical as is common in the western world, but adopts a kind of fervor common to the East.[122]

Sproul does believe that Christ will return, so he interprets Revelation 19 literally, but the rest of the book allegorically. Preterist Don Preston does not believe in any form of a second coming of Christ—holding instead that Jesus has already come back. In my opinion, this is outside the bounds of orthodox Christianity.

Preston also relies upon Revelation belonging to the apocalyptic category to find support for his view that Revelation's global language was fulfilled in the local events of A.D. 70. He observes that apocalyptic literature hyperbolizes the destruction of Jerusalem. According to Sibylline Oracle 5:153, "The whole creation was shaken" when war began on Jerusalem.[123] If Revelation is also apocalyptic literature, Preston here reasons that it too must be similarly using hyperbolic language.[124]

To Gentry, Sproul and Preston, the antichrist is not future, but the prophecies about him were fulfilled by Nero back in the first century.

Gentry states again:

> Before beginning my survey, I must note what most Christians suspect and what virtually all evangelical scholars (excluding classic dispensationalists) recognize regarding the book: Revelation is a highly figurative book that we cannot approach with a simple straightforward literalism.[125]

---

122 R. C. Sproul, *The Last Days According to Jesus* (Grand Rapids: Baker, 1998), p. 45.

123 Don Preston, *Who Is This Babylon?* (Don K. Preston, 1999), p. 98.

124 Ibid.

125 Gentry, *Four Views of Revelation*, p. 38.

I agree that the book is "highly figurative." However, we still interpret it literally, while also considering the book's many symbols and figures of speech when they are textually conscious (e.g., Rev. 8:8; 12:9; 17:8). By way of contrast, futurist Robert Thomas helps explain the preterist hermeneutic:

> A Preterist approach must assume an apocalyptic genre in which the language only faintly and indirectly reflects the actual events. This extreme allegorical interpretation allows for finding fulfillments in the first-century Roman Empire prior to the destruction of Jerusalem in A.D. 70.[126]

The emergent church is moving aggressively in this direction of preterism, as well. Brian McLaren states:

> The book of Revelation is an example of popular literary genre of ancient Judaism, known today as Jewish apocalyptic. Trying to read it without understanding its genre would be like watching *Star Trek* or some other science fiction show thinking it was a historical documentary . . . instead of being a book about the distant future, it becomes a way of talking about the challenges of the immediate present.[127]

Apparently, these interpreters, primarily emanating from the camp of Reformed Theology, see no problem in suspending the ordinary rules of hermeneutics, that were so carefully used by the reformers in retrieving the five solas, to get Revelation's global judgments to fit the historical and local events of A.D. 70.

126 Robert L. Thomas, "A Classical Dispensationalist View of Revelation," in *Four Views on the Book of Revelation*, ed. C. Marvin Pate (Grand Rapids: Zondervan, 1998), p. 181.

127 Brian McLaren, *The Secret Message of Jesus* (Nashville, TN: Word, 2006), pp. 175-76.

Reasons for Understanding 1,000 Literally

Yet, this disturbing pattern continues regarding how Reformed theologians approach numbers in the book of Revelation. For example, the 1,000-year kingdom is mentioned six times in Revelation 20:1-10. This leads us to believe that this is a reference to a literal 1,000 years. But some think that this conclusion is just too simplistic, so they consequently come up with a spiritualized or allegorized interpretation of the text. Gentry states:

> The proper understanding of the thousand-year time frame in Revelation 20 is that it is representative of a long and glorious era and is not limited to a literal 365,000 days. The figure represents a perfect cube of 10, which is the number of quantitative perfection.[128]

But is not seven the number of perfection in the Bible? When did it become 10?

And, if this passage is merely teaching that Jesus will reign for a long time, why did John not simply say that? He is quite capable of writing of indefinite concepts (cf. Rev. 20:3, 8).

Moreover, if we do not take this number 1,000 literally, this certainly casts doubt on the literal interpretation of specific numbers given throughout the rest of the book, including: four angels (7:1); 144,000 Jews (7:4); 12,000 from each tribe (7:5-8); seven angels (8:6); 42 months (11:2); two witnesses (11:3); 1,260 days (11:3); and 7,000 people (11:13).

Robert Thomas rightfully observes that "no number in Revelation is verifiably a symbolic number."[129]

Not only that, we learn by comparing these two quotations from Reformed commentator William Hendriksen that allegorization of the

128 Kenneth L. Gentry, *He Shall Have Dominion: A Post Millennial Eschatology* (Tyler, Texas: Institute for Christian economics, 1992), p. 335.

129 Robert Thomas, *Revelation 8 to 22: An Exegetical Commentary* (Chicago: Moody Press, 1992), p. 408.

numbers of years listed in Revelation leads to self-contradiction. Concerning Revelation 12:14, he writes:

> The expression "a time, and times, and half a time" occurs first in the book of Daniel 7:25; 12:7. It is the period of the antichrist. John emphasizes the fact that the spirit of the antichrist is in the world already (1 Jn. 4:3). In the Apocalypse *this period of three years and a half refers to the entire gospel age.*[130] (italics added)

Here Hedriksen contends that the *gospel age* is three-and-a-half years. Yet, notice how he contradicts himself in the same book just a few pages later. Concerning the 1,000 years mentioned six times in Revelation 20:1-10, he writes:

> In close harmony with all these scriptural passages—and our exegesis must always be based upon the analogy of Scripture—we conclude that here also in Revelation 20:1–3 the binding of Satan and the fact that he is hurled into the abyss to remain there for *a thousand years indicates that throughout this present gospel age* the devil's influence on earth is curtailed. He is unable to prevent the extension of the Church among the nations by means of an active missionary programme. During this entire period he is prevented from causing the nations—the world in general—to destroy the Church as a mighty, missionary institution.[131] (italics added)

The "gospel age" is three-and-a-half years . . . and also 1,000 years! Sadly, Hendriksen is dispensing with the literal method of interpretation that his very movement so carefully used to rescue the church in the area of the five *solas*.

Every number should be taken literally—unless you can demonstrate from the text itself that God intended it to be taken allegorically. There are

130 William Hendriksen, *More than Conquerors: An Interpretation of the Book of Revelation* (Grand Rapids, MI: Baker Books, 1967), p. 144.

131 Ibid., p. 188.

specific textual clues that tell us when this is the case. No such textual clue is applied in either of these instances.

The New Jerusalem

Consider the New Jerusalem—the city where the righteous will dwell, which is 1,500 miles cubed. It descends from heaven to the Earth. The saints are able to go in and out of the city, which is a little bigger than half of the continental United States. Here is John's description of the city:

> The city is laid out as a square, and its length is as great as the width; and he measured the city with the rod, fifteen hundred miles; its length and width and height are equal. And he measured its wall, seventy-two yards, *according to* human measurements, which are *also* angelic *measurements*. (Rev. 21:16-17)

God said that these measurements are actual, but Reformed theologians think that it is just crazy to take them literally. Note the following comments:

1. **Swete**: "Such dimensions defy imagination and are permissible only in the language of symbolism."[132]
2. **Barnes**: "Of course, this must preclude all idea of there being such a city literally in Palestine … this cannot be understood literally; and the very idea of a literal fulfillment of this shows the absurdity of that method of interpretation … this cannot be taken literally; and an attempt to explain all of this literally would show that that method of interpreting the Apocalypse is impracticable."[133]
3. **Grant**: "No clearer proof … that all is figurative. Such a height is simply out of harmony with the constitution of our world."[134]

---

132 Henry Barclay Swete, *The Apocalypse of St. John* (London: Macmillan, 1907), p. 289.

133 Albert Barnes, *Notes on the New Testament* (Grand Rapids, MI: Kregel, 1968), p. 1,722.

134 P.W. Grant, *The Revelation of John* (London: Hodder and Stoughton, 1889), p. 593. Swete,

4. **Boettner**: "Neither the shape nor the dimensions of the city can be taken with mathematical exactness, as if it were a gigantic apartment house."[135]

Such writers forget that John is talking about another world that is yet on the horizon—which is not based upon what is normal in this world.

Revelation 21:21 states:

> And the twelve gates were twelve pearls; each one of the gates was a single pearl. And the street of the city was pure gold, like transparent glass.

Progressive dispensationalists are those attempting to find a middle ground between traditional dispensationalism and covenant theology in their desire to build a bridge to Reformed theology. Progressive dispensationalism has been greatly influenced by Reformed theology.[136] Thus, it is not at all surprising to discover a similar de-literalized approach to the Apocalypse in the writings of prominent progressive dispensationalists. For example, progressive dispensationalist David Turner states:

> Perhaps the absence of oysters large enough to produce such pearls and the absence of sufficient gold to pave such a city (viewed literally 1380 miles squared and high) is viewed as sufficient reason not to take these images as fully literal! . . . the preceding discussion serves to warn against a "hyper-literal" approach to apocalyptic imagery. . . ."[137]

Thus, in Turner's mind, the description of the New Jerusalem cannot

---

Barnes and Grant quoted in Paul Lee Tan, *The Interpretation of Prophecy* (Winona Lake, IN: BMH, 1974; reprint, Dallas, TX: Paul Lee Tan Prophetic Ministries, 2015), pp. 285-86.

135 Loraine Boettner, *The Millennium* (Philadelphia, PA: Presbyterian and Reformed Publishing Company, 1958), p. 64.

136 Ryrie, *Dispensationalism*, pp. 167, 178.

137 David L. Turner, "The New Jerusalem in Revelation 21:1-22:5; Consummation of a Biblical Continuum," *Dispensationalism, Israel, and the Church,* ed., Craig A. Blaising and Darrell L. Bock (Grand Rapids: Zondervan, 1992), p. 277.

be literal since there are not enough oysters in the present world that are large enough to make pearls of such an enormous size. Nor is there enough gold in the present world for there to exist the streets of gold in the New Jerusalem as they are depicted in the book of Revelation, chapters 21 and 22. In fact, Turner goes so far as to castigate those who interpret such descriptions in their plain sense as "hyper-literal" in their hermeneutical approach. Yet, of course, God in His new creation can bring any of these into existence as He so desires.

Here is the classic definition of literal interpretation from David L. Cooper:

> When the plain sense of Scripture makes common sense, seek no other sense; therefore, take every word at its primary, ordinary, usual, literal meaning unless the facts of the immediate context, studied in light of related passages and axiomatic and fundamental truths, indicate clearly otherwise.[138]

We could tersely summarize Cooper's maxim by simply saying, "When the plain sense makes good sense seek no other sense lest you end up with nonsense."

Notice, however, that even when the book of Revelation speaks of something in highly symbolic language it still demands a literal interpretation. Sometimes the text even gives us that interpretation. Revelation 17:18 serves as a case in point:

> The woman whom you saw is the great city, which reigns over the kings of the earth.

The harlot described in Revelation 17 should not be construed as a literal harlot since Revelation 17:18 indicates that the harlot represents a city. However, without such an explicit textual clue provided, the "plain-sense"

138 David L. Cooper, *The World's Greatest Library Graphically Illustrated* (Los Angeles: Biblical Research Society, 1970), p. 11.

method of interpretation should be consistently followed when interpreting the book of Revelation. Yet, as has been demonstrated, the Reformed camp typically allegorizes the text of Revelation far beyond what is warranted.

Ezekiel 40–48

Finally, what about the temple in the millennial kingdom, which is described in detail, with its exact dimensions, in Ezekiel 40-48? Gary DeMar states:

> The Book of Hebrews was written to show beyond a shadow of a doubt that the entire Old Covenant system–with its priests, sacrifices, ceremonies, and temple–has been done away with in Christ. . . . The prophecy of Ezekiel's temple is a picture of the restored covenant community that returned to the land after the exile. The vision should not be projected 2500 years into the future into some earthly millennial kingdom where sacrifices will be offered *for atonement* in the presence of the crucified Christ.[139]

The problem with this view is that Ezekiel 8-11 describes an earlier temple. This earlier temple is the first Hebrew temple built by Solomon and ultimately destroyed by Nebuchadnezzar of Babylon. Thus, it was a literal temple. Both temples depicted in the book of Ezekiel are described with the same mathematical precision and detail. Why would one temple be literal and the other one not be literal? DeMar is interpreting the historical section of the book through one lens, and the eschatological section through another lens. Only through the imposition of a dual hermeneutic, one literal and the other allegorical, can he sustain his theology.

139 Gary DeMar, *Last Days Madness*, 4th rev. ed. (Powder Springs, GA: American, 1999), pp. 97-98.

The Central Problem

Here is the problem with failing to apply the literal approach to the entire Bible. It comes from Reformed theologian Albertus Pieters, given in 1931, and gets to the heart of the problem:

> The question whether the Old Testament prophecies concerning the people of God must be interpreted in their ordinary sense, as other Scriptures are interpreted, or can properly be applied to the Christian church, is called the question of spiritualization of prophecy. This is one of the major problems in biblical interpretation, and confronts everyone who makes a serious study of the Word of God. It is one of the chief keys to the difference of opinion between Premillenarians and the mass of Christian scholars. The former reject spiritualization, the latter employ it; and as long as there is no agreement on this point the debate is interminable and fruitless.[140]

As long as interpreters are employing different methods, they will reach different conclusions. Consistent literal interpretation is the fundamental issue. Because the Reformed tradition spawned by the Protestant Reformers has enshrined a dual hermeneutic, or a partially allegorical system of interpretation, it remains a fossilized system incapable of further reformation. Thus, it was necessary for God to use others outside of this tradition to further reform His church and thus rescue it from the allegorical Alexandrian influence that held sway in the church throughout the Middle Ages. Bernard Ramm well notes:

> The allegorical system that arose among the pagan Greeks, copied by the Alexandrian Jews, was next adopted by the Christian church and largely dominated exegesis until the Reformation, with such notable exceptions as the Syrian school of Antioch. . . .[141]

140 Albertus Pieters, "The leader," Sept. 5, 1831; as cited in John F. Walvoord, *The Millennial Kingdom: A Basic Text in Premillennial Theology* (Findlay, OH: Dunham, 1959), p. 128.

141 Bernard Ramm, *Protestant Biblical Interpretation*, 3rd rev. ed. (Grand Rapids: Baker, 1970), p. 28.

While the Protestant Reformers made at least a dent in this allegorical armor through their use of selective literalism to retrieve the five *solas*, as we have noted, the Reformers did not go far enough. Consequently, the traditions that they began remain literal in some parts of the Bible but largely allegorical in other areas. Therefore, God would have to raise up others to complete the task begun by the Reformers. Those that God used in this regard will become the subject of the next chapter.

CHAPTER 7

Dispensationalism and the Completed Revolution

The Reformed movement, as I have explained it, is almost incapable of developing further progress. It is stuck in the same place it has been since the day the Protestant Reformers left the scene—utilizing literal interpretation to a point, and then reverting to an allegorical interpretation in other places (especially in the area of eschatology).

But God did something to complete the revolution begun by the Protestant Reformers. Although He continued to use men and women within the Reformed movement, He also reached outside the Reformed movement to finish the job that the Reformers started.

You see, Reformed theology today remains in a state of incompletion—like a half-baked meal.

The Reformers rescued the church from allegorization *in some areas*—for which we praise and thank the Lord. They did this heroically, at great risk to their own personal lives, and we owe them a tremendous debt of gratitude.

Yet they also left other parts of the Bible steeped in allegorization.

But God raised up others—with the dawning of the dispensational movement of the 19th century.

The Reformed movement deserves much credit, because they had the right tool—the literal method of interpretation—which they used to rescue the church in the area of the five *solas*. The downfall is that they applied this correct tool to only some of the Bible.

The good news is that we still have that tool! Dispensationalists have taken that tool and used it to further and complete the work of the Protestant Reformers. There is a Scriptural principle involved here in this building process. By way of analogy, let us consider the words of the Apostle Paul in 1 Corinthians 3:10:

> According to the grace of God which was given to me, like a wise master builder I laid a foundation, and another is building on it. But each man must be careful how he builds on it.

Dispensationalists took the Reformers' hermeneutic, and desired to apply it to the entire Bible.

What is Literal Interpretation?

Now, what exactly do we mean by literal interpretation? Bernard Ramm answers, showing what the Reformers retrieved from the school of Antioch and gave to us: A literal hermeneutic attaches to every word the same meaning that it would have in normal usage, whether employed in speaking, writing or thinking.[142]

The key, of course, is to understand the meaning that a word or words had in Biblical times. The interpreter is trying to put himself or herself in the position of the original audience and learn how they would comprehend these terms.

After all, God's goal in His Word was to communicate with mankind. This communication is muted when we apply our own meanings to it.

Apostolic, Antiochene and Reformation hermeneutical methodology

142 Bernard, *Ramm, Protestant Biblical Interpretation* (Boston: W.A. Wilde, 1956), pp. 89-92.

can best be described as the literal, grammatical, historical, contextual method of interpretation. Let us break these adjectives down and consider each of them in greater detail.

Literal Interpretation

According to the etymology of the word, *literal* means "by the letters."[143]

Thus, when you interpret the Bible literally you are reading what is there—rather than bringing external baggage with you into the text and re-interpreting what is there.

Grammatical Interpretation

Grammar matters! God sovereignly chose to inspire and record the Old Testament mostly in Hebrew (and a little Aramaic) and the New Testament entirely in Greek.

We must study these original languages, paying attention to the rules of grammar for each—including syntax and sentence structure. Once a message becomes encapsulated in linguistic form, it is governed by the laws of language. There are laws of language, just as there are laws of mathematics and science. Language functions according to laws.

Historical Interpretation

Each book of the Bible was written in a historical context. Take the letter to the Ephesians, for instance. Paul wrote it from Rome to the church at Ephesus. Now, in order to understand this book, we would want to learn when Paul wrote it, as well as how its first recipients understood history and language.

You are, in essence, transporting yourself backward in time in an

143 See "literal (adj.)" at https://www.etymonline.com/word/literal; Internet; accessed 19 November 2017.

attempt to learn what actually happened there. You want to learn how the original recipients of the book would have understood it.

Contextual Interpretation

We are trying to read the Scriptures in their original context. We are not just piecing things together—that do not belong together—from various parts of the Bible.

This helps us to interpret a passage such as Matthew 5:29-30:

> If your right eye makes you stumble, tear it out and throw it from you; for it is better for you to lose one of the parts of your body, than for your whole body to be thrown into hell. If your right hand makes you stumble, cut it off and throw it from you; for it is better for you to lose one of the parts of your body, than for your whole body to go into hell.

Is Jesus literally telling us to cut out our eyes? The answer to that is no—based on the context. Here, in the Sermon on the Mount, Christ is not addressing the issue of severed body parts. Rather, He is addressing issues of the heart. His central point is that the sins of adultery and murder manifest themselves in the human heart. Because Christ's ultimate emphasis in the Sermon on the Mount is the human heart (cf. Matt. 5:21-22, 27-28), gouging out one's eyes obviously would not stop such sins from occurring since they are ultimately sourced in the heart. Even without one's eyes it is possible to mentally fantasize about committing both adultery and murder. In this way, Christ is using a figure of speech called *hyperbole* (the use of a deliberate exaggeration to communicate an idea). Jesus is speaking here in a symbolic sense about the necessity of dealing drastically with sin.

After you as an interpreter have done all of this work, then you must develop your application. You must consider how the truth that you have studied applies to your own life, or how you as a teacher could apply it to the lives of others.

This is what the school of Antioch was teaching for the first two centuries of church history—and what was lost, and what the Reformers reclaimed in certain areas relative to the five *solas*.

The Straw Man Fallacy

The straw man fallacy is where you misrepresent your opponent's position, then tear down that misrepresentation. It is a logical fallacy because you are not dealing with what your opponent is actually saying, but rather with your misrepresentation of it.

As literal interpreters, we get a straw man thrown at us all of the time. The charge is that we do not believe in figures of speech. We are told that we believe that "the mountains sing" (Ps. 98:8) and "the trees of the field . . . clap *their* hands" (Isa. 55:12).

The fact of the matter is that every literal interpreter makes room for figures of speech.

Thus, according to Charles Ryrie, literal interpretation:

> . . . might also be called plain interpretation so that no one receives the mistaken notion that the literal principle rules out figures of speech. Symbols, figures of speech, and types . . . are in no way contrary to literal interpretation.[144]

Within language, you can communicate either literally or figuratively. When the intention of communicator is literal interpretation, such communication is sometimes referred to as *denotative* communication. When the communicator wants to be understood figurately, such communication is often referred to as *connotative* communication.[145] The inherent danger of

144 Charles C. Ryrie, *Dispensationalism Today* (Chicago: Moody Press, 1965), p. 87.

145 Elliott E. Johnson, *Expository Hermeneutics: An Introduction* (Grand Rapids: Academie Books, 1990), pp. 44, 307-8.

any interpretation is interpreting words or phrases connotatively when they are meant to be understood denotatively or, conversely, interpreting them denotatively when they are meant to be understood connotatively. To avoid this error, a general good rule of thumb to follow is to interpret the text in a denotative or literal sense unless the writer provides a clear, conspicuous textual clue, thereby signaling his intention to be understood figuratively or connotatively.

E.W. Bullinger (1837-1913) identified every possible figure of speech you can have in the whole Bible. His book, *Figures of Speech Used in the Bible*, is still the standard text on this subject.[146]

When someone throws this straw man at you, think of Bullinger. While I do not agree with all his conclusions, he certainly stood for literal interpretation, and also understood figures of speech. Literal interpreters are very sensitive to figures of speech.

We always need to be aware of such figures of speech, and ask ourselves if the author desires to be understood literally or figuratively. Generally speaking, when a Biblical author desires to be understood figuratively, he will give you a clue.

Notice Galatians 4:24 as it discusses Sarah and Hagar:

> This is *allegorically* speaking, for these *women* are two covenants: one *proceeding* from Mount Sinai bearing children who are to be slaves; she is Hagar. (first italics added)

Now, when we are reading in the book of Genesis, we take the characters *Sarah* and *Hagar* literally. But here in the New Testament, the Apostle Paul uses them to develop a spiritual idea.

Notice, I am not free, of my own accord, to go through the Bible and assign allegorical interpretations to historical events just as I desire. I may not do this unless the text tells me to do so. Paul has done this at the beginning of

146 E. W. Bullinger, *Figures of Speech Used in the Bible Explained and Illustrated* (London: Eyre and Spottiswoode, 1898; reprint, Grand Rapids: Baker Book House, 1968).

the verse above through his employment of the term "allegorically." He wants his words to be understood in a figurative sense, and thus gives us permission to take them that way. When the Bible gives us such permission, it will also give us the very interpretation of the allegory. I am not free to interpret the allegory in any way that I want, based on my own sanctified imagination. I must follow the interpretation that the text gives.

Here is another example from the book of Revelation, related to the two witnesses of the tribulation period:

> And their dead bodies *will lie* in the street of the great city which *mystically* is called Sodom and Egypt, where also their Lord was crucified. (Rev. 11:8; italics added in the second line)

The *great city* here is identified as Jerusalem—"where also their Lord was crucified." But the Apostle John desired to add more meaning to his statement. His use of the term *mystically* makes this intention apparent. He calls the city *Sodom*, which represents moral depravity, and *Egypt*, which represents bondage. In other words, the literal city of Jerusalem is shown—through these figures of speech—to be out of fellowship with God. It is an unbelieving city at this time, a place where the antichrist kills these two witnesses. Yet, John's intention to allegorize in this matter is communicated to the reader through his use of the term *mystically*. Absent this expression, no such excursions into allegorical interpretation would be permissible according to literal interpretation.

When we practice literal interpretation consistently from Genesis to Revelation, we are allowing the authority to remain in the text. When we deviate from that and spiritualize things that are not meant to be interpreted spiritually, then the authority over the interpretive process is transferred from the text to the mind of the interpreter. The issue is really, "Who is in control?" I want to enthrone the Word of God as the authority. After all, God gave us His Word—who am I to rewrite God?

Horatius Bonar (1808–1889) best summarizes the meaning of literal interpretation as provided in the following important quotation, which is introduced in the writing of Charles Feinberg:

> Probably as valuable a testimony as any that could be offered was given by Dr. Horatius Bonar. When speaking of the results of fifty years of the study of prophecy, he concluded with the statement that first of all, he had gained assurance as to the authority and inspiration of the Scriptures. Secondly, he felt more certain than ever that the literal interpretation of the Word is the best. Said he: "'literal if possible,' is, I believe the only maxim that will carry you right through the Word of God from Genesis to Revelation."[147]

The Dawning of the Dispensational Movement

God raised up a new movement—the dispensational movement, beginning in the 19th century—and its leaders began to do what the Reformers and their spiritual descendants had not done. They began to apply the literal method of interpretation to the whole Bible. The dispensational movement thus retrieved key doctrines, which had been lost due to allegorization, from the Bible. They were acting in the same way as the Reformers, who used this methodology to begin to retrieve doctrines, which had been lost due to allegorization, from the Bible. The Reformers primarily retrieved the *solas*. Among the teachings that the dispensationalists retrieved were chiliasm, the Israel-church distinction and pretribulationalism.

147 Horatius Bonar, quoted in Charles L. Feinberg, *Millennialism: The Two Major Views* (Winona Lake, IN: BMH, 1985), pp. 47-48.

Chiliasm

The dispensationalists began to study the Abrahamic covenant and see that it is both unconditional and unfulfilled. Therefore, they reasoned, since God cannot lie (Tit. 1:2), there must be a future kingdom whereby the language of the covenant will be literally fulfilled. This develops into premillennialism—which the school of Antioch had taught for the first two centuries of the church. The dispensationalists consistently reversed Alexandrianism, and took us all the way back to Antioch.

They saw that the land, seed and blessings promises of the Abrahamic covenant in Genesis 15 are further clarified in the land covenant of Deuteronomy 29 and 30 (*land*); the Davidic covenant in 2 Samuel 7:12-16 (*seed*); and the new covenant in Jeremiah 31:31-34 (*blessing*).

The Israel–Church Distinction

The dispensationalists also saw Israel and the church as being different—two separate peoples and programs. This insight placed a curb on anti-Semitism. After all, why should we hate the Jews when a literal reading of the Bible reveals that God has a special future in store for them? Consistent literal interpretation also hindered the types of social and political experiments that had been done in places like Geneva, as well as earlier through the crusades and the Spanish Inquisition. Our method of interpretation rescued the church from those terrible social experiments. Why is this so? It is because in order to get those to work you must take the Mosaic law and the Old Testament and apply these Scriptures—intended for Israel—to the church, in a metaphorical sense. Literal interpretation rules out such misapplications of Biblical truth since the Mosaic Law was designed only for national Israel (cf. Ps. 147:19-20).

As another case in point, the unbelieving Jews in Israel today love dispensationalists. They recognize that we are a massive force in the United States that is very pro-Israel. We believe that Israel has a purpose and a role in history, and a right to her land. We derive these concepts from a consistently literal interpretation of the Bible.

These emphases also keep the church focused on what it is supposed to be doing—which is carrying out the Great Commission that our Lord gave to us in Matthew 28:18-20.

Pre-Tribulation Rapture

Such developments in doctrine also led to a widespread understanding of the pretribulational rapture—a special aspect of the second coming of Christ that is unique for all church-age believers. This Israel–church distinction, in turn, informs the church that she cannot be in Israel's tribulation period leading to her conversion (cf. Jer. 30:7), since this concept represents God's work through Israel rather than the church. All of this to say that the aforementioned Israel–church distinction provides a proper foundation for embracing a pre-tribulational rapture.

These doctrines had been lying dormant—and continue to be so in Reformed theology. They began to re-emerge through the influence of the dispensationalists, just as the five *solas* re-emerged through the influence of the Reformers.

Key Literal Interpreters

Some key commentators were instrumental in this process. Among the most prominent are the following:

1. John Nelson Darby (1800–1882)
2. Sir Robert Anderson (1841–1918)

3. Cyrus Ingerson Scofield (1843–1921)
4. William Eugene Blackstone (1841–1935)
5. Henry Allen Ironside (1876–1951)
6. Lewis Sperry Chafer (1871–1952)

Darby is probably most responsible—through the application of consistent literalism—for retrieving the Israel-church distinction, as well as its corollary doctrine, the pre-tribulational rapture, from the Scriptures.

Anderson specifically rediscovered the meaning of the 70 weeks of Daniel 9 and unlocked their secrets. He taught us that if the first 69 weeks were fulfilled literally, then the remaining week will also be fulfilled literally. He said:

> There is not a single prophecy, of which the fulfillment is recorded in Scripture, that was not realized with absolute accuracy, and in every detail; and it is wholly unjustifiable to assume that a new system of fulfillment was inaugurated after the sacred canon closed. . . . Literalness of fulfillment may therefore be accepted as an axiom to guide us in the study of prophecy.[148]

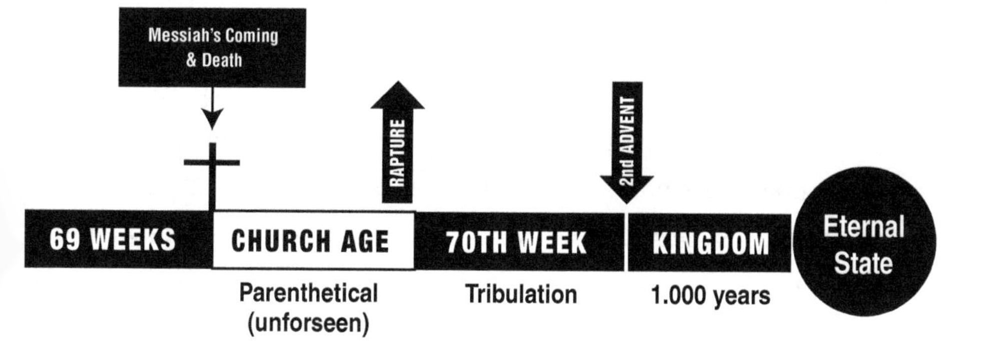

148 Robert Anderson, *The Coming Prince*, 2nd rev. ed. (London: Hodder and Stoughton, 1882; reprint, Grand Rapids: Kregel, 1957), pp. 147-48.

Scofield gave us the *Scofield Reference Bible.*[149] It is difficult to overestimate the impact made by the Scofield Bible, because it put the Bible into the hands of the laity in a powerful new way. It gave them a Bible with doctrinal footnotes at the bottom of the pages. This made the literal interpretation of the Bible accessible to average people through those explanatory notes. While we may not agree with every single note, we recognize that those notes guided churchmen who could see their mainline denominations going liberal in the early and middle decades of the 20th century. When they heard things in sermons that did not ring true Biblically, they could check them against the notes in their Scofield Bibles.

Blackstone wrote a popular book about the return of Christ entitled *Jesus is Coming*. In it, he even drew attention to the significance of the nation of Israel roughly four decades *before* Israel was reborn nationally in 1948. He noted:

> Israel is God's sun dial. If anyone desires to know our place in God's chronology, our position in the great march of events, look at Israel.[150]

Lewis Sperry Chafer wrote many books, including a dispensationally based *Systematic Theology.*[151] He was also the founder of Dallas Theological Seminary, which became the leading dispensational institution of higher learning in the 20th century.

There were many other such things that God used this powerful surge of dispensational teachers to accomplish. Like the Reformers before them, they built upon a foundation that they had been given, then passed their tools on to the next generation—for them to continue the building effort.

May God help us to carry on the faithful legacy of both the Reformers and the dispensationalists!

---

149 C. I. Scofield, ed. *The New Scofield Reference Bible* (New York: Oxford University, 1909; reprint, 1996).

150 *Jesus Is Coming: God's Hope for a Restless World* (New York: F.H. Revell, 1908; reprint, Grand Rapids: Kregel, 1989), p. 238.

151 Lewis Sperry Chafer, *Systematic Theology*, 8 vols. (Dallas: Dallas Seminary, 1948; reprint, [8 vols. in 4], Grand Rapids: Kregel, 1993).

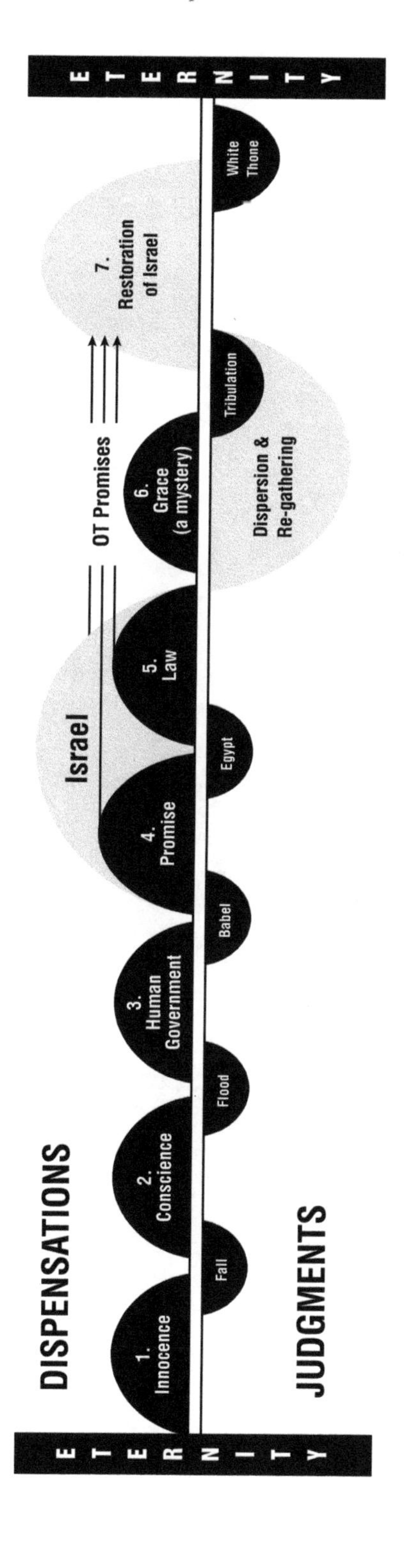
ETERNITY
DISPENSATIONS
JUDGMENTS
1. Innocence
Fall
2. Conscience
Flood
3. Human Government
Babel
4. Promise
Egypt
Israel
5. Law
OT Promises
6. Grace (a mystery)
Tribulation
Dispersion & Re-gathering
7. Restoration of Israel
White Thone
ETERNITY

CHAPTER 8

Looking Back 500 Years Later

How do we properly look at the Protestant Reformation for our vantage point today?

We rejoice over the Reformers and should be grateful for them, although we do not idolize them. But we are thankful for all that they accomplished and the price that they paid—some of them paying with their own lives.

We also understand that the restoration that they led was very partial. It was very important, but was not complete.

What they restored to us—from an ancient toolbox—was the tool, or the methodology, of literal interpretation.

Why did the Reformers not complete their hermeneutical revolution? Part of the answer may be simply that they got old and tired. They accomplished so much in their lifetimes—it was almost a super-human feat. To expect them to have done more may not be realistic. We must also realize that they carried much baggage with them from Catholicism into the Reformation. Remember—they had initially hoped to remain Catholic!

Also, remember that they were just people—just people that God used in a specific area. We have to understand them in the context in which they lived so that we can properly and fully learn from them.

Some would argue that the Reformation is really of no value at all to those of us who are dispensationalists, evangelicals or fundamentalists, but I cannot accept that. I have a hard time believing any Christian group that claims some type of direct lineage that goes straight back to the apostles, bypassing the Reformation. All of us are standing on the shoulders of the Reformers in one way or another.

I do realize that God has always had a remnant—and many of us would like to think that the particular Christian group to which we belong was a part of the remnant. Given all the historical forces that were at work during the Dark Ages, however, it is very difficult for me to see any kind of significant line of faithful Christians that goes all the way back to the apostles and remained free from the Roman Catholic Church. We are all building on a foundation that the Reformers set down beneath us.

Yet God is so good, and loves His church so much, that He raised up other people to complete the work that the Reformers began, and to do what they could not do.

God has indeed raised up people, since the 19th century, to take the Reformational hermeneutic—which is really the apostolic and Antiochian hermeneutic—and apply it to the entire Bible. We call these people *dispensationalists.*

The field of eschatology, the study of the end times, was the last major area of systematic theology to be systematized. The church had already systematized theology proper, Christology, the atonement, salvation, the doctrines of grace and many other areas. But it was not really not until the 1800s that Christians began to systematize eschatology. This is the outworking of the concept of progressive illumination. We are sitting here today on top of all of these wonderful doctrines that we just take for granted—not really understanding how it took the church centuries to formally systematize all of these areas.

One of the tools that the Lord has used to get the church to systematize truth was the presence of heretics, such as Arius in the days of the Nicene Council. While heretics may appear to be a threat to the church, often they have the positive effect of forcing the church to do some hard thinking (cf. 1 Cor. 11:19).

One interesting dynamic to note along these lines is that dispensational theologians have faithfully read and studied the writings of Reformed theologians, but the reverse is seldom true. Thus, Reformed theologians often mischaracterize our beliefs.

One final takeaway that is worthy of emphasizing again is that many people today in the emergent church are attempting to go back to the darkness of the Middle Ages—even leapfrogging the Reformation and seeking for truth that was supposedly lost in the Reformation. They want to retrieve information from the pre-Reformation Dark Ages. When people do this, they demonstrate that their authority base is outside of the Scriptures.

The trajectory of my life has been the opposite. In my life, I have gone from a mainline Protestant background that focused on experiences such as liturgy, candles, bells, holy water and the stations of the cross to a focus on the study of the Bible. Sadly, many even in Bible churches today are going in the other direction. It is a Scripture-plus-history mentality. They are looking for truth that they believe was lost subsequent to the Reformation that will help them experience Christianity in a new way.

The emergent church has all but rid itself of any type of authoritative Bible teaching. They are turning back to the very things from which the Reformers helped us to escape. It is a reversal of *sola Scriptura*.

Friends, let us celebrate this 500th anniversary of the Protestant Reformation by proclaiming the Word of God as our authority, rather than church tradition. The Apostle Paul specifically warned us that church history would be dominated by spiritually *savage wolves* (Acts. 20:29).

We must *be on guard* (Acts 20:28) against this very same danger in our own generation. We could lose everything if we do not remain vigilant, with the Lord's help. We cannot let that happen. We must be diligent to defend the truth and hand it off to the next generation. Understanding history will help us greatly toward that end. Studying church history helps us, so that we do not make the same errors over again.

May God give us the courage and strength of the Reformers as we continue to serve Christ and His church—*Ever Reforming*!

I hope that this book has helped you toward that noble and glorious end.

Dispensational Publishing House is striving to become the go-to source for Bible-based materials from the dispensational perspective.

Our goal is to provide high-quality doctrinal and worldview resources that make dispensational theology accessible to people at all levels of understanding.

Visit our blog regularly to read informative articles from both known and new writers.

And please let us know how we can better serve you.

Dispensational Publishing House, Inc.
PO Box 3181
Taos, NM 87571

Call us toll free 844-321-4202

CPSIA information can be obtained
at www.ICGtesting.com
Printed in the USA
LVHW01s1609120918
589925LV00026B/648/P